THE WAGER

THE WAGER

a play in three acts By

Mark Medoff

JAMES T. WHITE & COMPANY
Clifton, New Jersey

for

My Mother   *My Father*   *My Brother*

The Wager was first presented by Richard Lee Marks, Henry Jaffe and William Craver at the Eastside Playhouse, in New York City, on October 21, 1974. It was directed by Anthony Perkins, the scenery was designed by David Mitchell; the lighting was designed by Neil Peter Jampolis; and the costume co-ordinator was Mary Beth Regan. The cast, in order of appearance, was as follows:

LEEDS ....Kristoffer Tabori
WARD ....Kenneth Gilman
HONOR ....Linda Cook (later, Carolyn Hurlburt)
RON ....John Heard

(Originally produced by the HB Playwrights Foundation Workshop Series.)

PLACE: A university in northern California, the apartment of two graduate students.

TIME: The present.

ACT I

SCENE 1: Thursday evening.
SCENE 2: Seventeen minutes later.

ACT II

Late Friday afternoon.

ACT III

SCENE 1: Seconds later.
SCENE 2: Saturday morning.

THE CHARACTERS:

LEEDS: *Sugar Pops?*

WARD: *Justify nothing to no one . . . Just do!*

HONOR: *My life mustn't be pledged to anything or anybody against my will if I can do anything to prevent it.*

RON: *I don't know anything. Except that I love my wife and I don't want to lose her.*

PREFACE

When I reflect on *The Wager* now, several months after its "official" run at the Eastside Playhouse in New York ended, I think of it with an elusive and maddening (because of its elusiveness, perhaps) sense of some ultimate *dys*-: dysphoria, dysthymia, and certainly dyspepsia all come to mind.

I was twenty-six when I wrote the first version of *The Wager*. It was a long one-act play consisting of ten scenes. I recognized that both Leeds and Ward were me, at war with each other; I recognized Ron and Honor Stevens; I recognized a driving force steeped in my own desires, fears, guilts, indiscretions. I loved the play passionately and I thought it monstrously funny, signaling the advent of a particular kind of humor I've continued to create, I think, in most of my work since: humor wrung out of things that really aren't a damn bit funny.

In March of 1967, *The Wager* was performed here in Las Cruces, New Mexico, where I was then an instructor of English at New Mexico State University, fresh out of graduate school at Stanford. I don't remember a whole lot about the process. I didn't do very much rewriting, I remember, and I intruded a lot into the directoral process when I was least welcome. The actor who played Leeds had to learn his lines in something less than forty-eight hours without benefit of being able to look at them— I recall that very well. He had been cast originally in the part, had discovered two days into rehearsal that he had a detached retina in one eye, and had left immediately for San Francisco and an operation. His replacement fell off a couch during rehearsal two days before the play was to start its two-night run, displaced something in his back from its intended position, and was replaced by the original actor, back from his eye operation but wearing little goggles with a pinhole in the center of each lens. The pinholes were the only visual connection between him and the outside world and one of the stipulations in wearing the goggles was that he was not to read anything. This extraordinary actor, Bill Frankfather, went on, goggles and all, and played Leeds as well as anybody ever has.

The joy of seeing a play I had written performed by a

group of living actors before a living audience was far more incredible than I can begin to say now, eight years and a lot of cynicism later.

In part because I assured him he would love the place, Frankfather went to Stanford to work for an MFA in Drama. The time came in late 1968 when he asked me if he could do *The Wager* as a directing project out there. I exhumed the play, read it, still loved it, and at Bill's urging, expanded it to full length (two acts at that time). He directed the play and played Leeds a second time, this time without the goggles. The reception was such that he was asked to remount the play the following school year for a longer run. Between the productions, I did a good deal of rewriting, working mostly on Honor and on the elimination of extraneous—but very wonderful, naturally—business (such as that involving the unseen character known only as "the guy who saw Honor's psychiatrist the hour after Honor saw her psychiatrist," whose unfortunate end it was to drink a vial of sulphuric acid in unrequited love of her).

In January of 1971, another friend from Las Cruces, Richard Carlson, the original Leonard in *Doing a Good One for the Red Man*, directed *The Wager* in Albuquerque, just as he had directed or would eventually direct *Red Man, The War on Tatem*, and *The Froegle Dictum* there for me. The play was still in two acts and pretty much as it had been for the second Stanford production. The thing that Richard and I recall most vividly about that production is that the actress who played Honor is a person neither of us has ever laid eyes on since, a fact for which both of us remain grateful.

In 1972 Ken Frankel, who would direct *When You Comin Back, Red Ryder?* a year later and with whom I got together initially because his cousin is my former dentist, did a reading production of *The Wager* at The Cubiculo in New York. The actors sat around a table and almost outnumbered the audience, but nevertheless I felt for the first time that my arrival on the Big Scene was imminent.

Following the Cubiculo production, the play was *supposed* to receive a production of some sort in New York where the actors rose from the table, Ken directing, me in attendance. So, in November of that year, I ended up directing the play in Miami. The fact that Miami is a thousand miles from New York aside, the experience was terrific. Directing the play forced me to look at it with an eye I would not have used had I continued simply as the playwright. The play was enormously successful critically and we ran for three months.

Enter the play's first Real Producer, who arranged a production in New York at the HB Playwrights Foundation in Greenwich Village in the winter of 1973. Like the working experience in Miami, this too was a joyous time. It was an experience for my wife Stephanie and me utterly unlike what we had anticipated (negative, terrifying, difficult). Frank Geraci, the director, and the actors, Craig Heller (who had played Ward for me in Miami), Arthur Taxier, Martha Ritter, and George Hosmer, were people with whom we felt a moving intimacy, people whom we still consider monumental in our lives, and friends. The play changed quite a lot during the rehearsal period there. Honor continued to grow and the relationship between her and Leeds began to dominate more than the relationship between Leeds and Honor's husband, Ron, which was my original concern in the first thirty or forty versions of the play.

At the Manhattan Theatre Club in 1974, the atmosphere had about it an electricity that, rather than merely sparking magic, threatened electrocution. The initial circumstances were unfortunate: the producer who had the option on *The Wager*, who had arranged the HB Playwrights Foundation production and a Manhattan Theatre Club production, was on his way out and a group of three producers was on its way in. Caught in the middle was the Manhattan Theatre Club, which irrespective of all the hard feelings that were to follow, wanted nothing but the best for me and for my play. Three actors and a director were fired. The production opened to the public but not to the press and, instead of moving intact as *Red Ryder* had to a larger theater, it closed down, to be begun from zero again in the fall. It was an agonizing experience for a lot of people, too many people. Friendships were mutilated, others tested, ideals squashed, the simple reality of New York's "Bust or Boom" theatrical syndrome made abundantly clear to all of us—including me—to whom it wasn't priorly clear. I am not proud to say that a handful of bodies lay strewn between the Manhattan Theatre Club on East Seventy-third Street and the Eastside Playhouse, where the play opened officially several months later, on East

Seventy-fourth Street, their back walls connected like Siamese twins.

On a positive note, however, there was a period of a month where those two connected theaters, the Eastside Playhouse and the Manhattan Theatre Club, were both playing plays of mine —*Red Ryder* and *The Wager*—and many a night Stephanie and I walked round and round the block, glorying in our good fortune and, needless to say, my genius.

When *The Wager* went back into rehearsal in the fall of 1974, two actors from the Manhattan Theatre Club production were retained, two Leedses were fired and finally replaced by the Manhattan Theatre Club production's second Leeds. The tar on the cake was that eventually the Honor who went into rehearsal for the Eastside Playhouse production was replaced a month into the run by her understudy.

Though the collaboration among my producers, toward whom I developed and maintain very strong familial feelings, Tony Perkins, the director, and me was always stimulating and positive, I had reached a point with the play, this play, which I didn't reach with *Red Ryder*, and haven't with any of the others. I was sick of rewriting it—even though the very most of the rewriting created material that was better than what I had before. I was tired of talking about what the play was trying to be; I was eight years older than I was when I had the initial need to write it—I didn't *know* what it was trying to be anymore because it had already *been* what it needed to be.

Consequently, I found myself *aiming* the play at a market. And mind you, I do not confess that that was evil, immoral, prostitutional. I didn't even give much thought to the fact that I was being terribly grown-up and pragmatic as hell. *I was tired of thinking about this wonderfully funny, moving play with its enormously original characters—period.* I wanted the beloved bastard off my back. I wanted it and the people who owned the production rights to it and the actors who would hopefully reap a harvest from their hard-wrung performances to somehow *excuse me* from further obligations.

When the play finally opened, anything would have seemed an anti-climax, and did.

Whereas, when *Red Ryder* moved to the Eastside Playhouse from the Circle Repertory Theatre, I could rarely resist stopping in to watch the audience arrive or leave, to watch a little bit of a performance, to *hang around* this thing I had conceived, opening night of *The Wager* at the Eastside—after eight years, its *official* opening—was the last I saw of it.

I sometimes hope that some graduate student someday doing a doctoral dissertation in some arcane combination of disciplines like geography, criminology, and lit will be foolish enough to undertake a study in dementia based on the eight-year odyssey of *The Wager* from the Las Cruces Community Theater, where a man in goggles played Leeds on two-days' notice, to the Eastside Playhouse, where on opening night, Tony Perkins, in an effort to ease both of our nerves, wore throughout the second act of *The Wager* to my immense enjoyment a pair of plastic vampire teeth.

I guess the worst of it is the feeling that some very definite part of my experience, my consciousness spent eight years being eased and bumped here and there like some very much alive and growing but aging deterministic . . . *thing*—and I just resent the *hell* out of that for my play and for me. Only slightly less acidic than that is the knowledge that the American theater—if it *ever* did—does not now exist nearly so much for the benefit of the people who grow it as for the people who eat it. Those two things, in the final analysis, are enough to generate not only dysphoria, dysthymia, and dyspepsia but a whacking good case of dysuria for the cold, lonely nights.

Ultimately, of course, beyond all of this external agony, nausea, and bladder trouble, there is an unquenchable love of writing for the theater and an immitigable narcissism about what I write. It is these feelings that prevail—a fact for which I am considerably more than grateful.

ACT ONE

*The living room of an apartment belonging to two gradu-
ate students. The furnishings are random and eclectic.
Downstage center is a spool table flanked by a modern can-
vas armchair and by a director's chair with the word "coach"
on the back.*

*Stage right is Ward's area which is dominated by athletic
equipment. Downstage right is a toy box which contains a
basketball, a football, a small leather-bound notebook, a
baseball glove, a baseball, and other jock items. A pyramid
of Little League bats is nearby. Above the toy box hangs a
dart board. Two small dumbbells sit beside the toy box.
Against the stage right wall is an old daybed couch which is
partially covered by an afghan. Above the couch is a window with venetian blinds, through which can be seen another impersonal apartment building.*

*On the upstage wall and above the couch are shelves con-
taining various athletic trophies and pictures. A small wall
lamp illuminates the head of the couch. Upstage right is a
door to the bedroom, through which can be seen twin beds,
a dresser, a portable television, and the door to the bathroom. Posters hang on the bedroom walls. On the center of
the upstage wall hangs a bulletin board with newspaper
clippings and more athletic pictures. Above the bulletin
board is a basketball hoop and net; the hoop is only seven
feet off the floor. Below the hoop, a large wooden Little
League scoreboard leans against the wall. Upstage center
is a small hallway leading to the front door. There is a coat
closet in the hallway. Upstage left is an open kitchen area,
in front of which is a kitchen counter with two bar stools.
In the kitchen are a practical refrigerator and the sort of
shelves and counters which are standard in modern apart-
ments.*

*Against the stage left wall is Leeds' area. Whereas the ath-
letic area has a certain neatness and symmetry, this section
of the room is impersonal and seemingly purposely di-*

sheveled. Leeds' desk is an old door atop two metal file cabinets and is covered with dirty dishes, pipe smoking paraphernalia, open books, and scraps of paper. Above the desk are bookshelves which are precariously overloaded. A gooseneck drafting lamp illuminates the desk.

As the curtain rises, a single spotlight picks out a small blackboard on an easel. Standing beside it is Leeds—a man who seems purposely careless in his dress and, more importantly, a man who enters a room and by his gaze makes the inhabitants of the room uneasy. His gaze is fixed on the audience; this is his room, his theater, his play. He wears a turtleneck sweater with a shoulder holster and revolver strapped over it. A dangerous explosiveness rages beneath his very cool exterior. He focuses on the audience and "lectures" at them his opening speech. His intent in this speech does not seem so much to help the audience understand where the play will begin but to let the audience know who he is and who they are in relation to him.

LEEDS: (*Illustrating his lecture on the blackboard.*)

When Honor Stevens' husband

(*Drawing an "S" in upper right corner of blackboard.*)

started down toward the pool,

(*Drawing an oval to represent the pool in lower center of blackboard.*)

Ward

(*Drawing a "W" in upper left.*)

suggested to Honor

(*Placing an "H" beside the "W."*)

that he had better go,

(*Drawing dots from the "W" to the corner of the blackboard.*)

hoping to insinuate to her that either more existed between them than did,

(*Drawing a line connecting the "W" and the "H."*)

or that he was fully aware of what she was fully aware of:

(*Drawing a heart around the "W" and "H."*)

that there existed between them more than her husband suspected.

(*Drawing an arrow through the heart.*)

And by leaping up when young Professor Stevens came onto the patio and diving hastily into the pool,

(*Drawing a line from the "W" to the pool.*)

Ward hoped to suggest to Stevens that he didn't want Stevens to suspect that anything existed between him and his wife because that's exactly what he hoped to suggest. Ward swam forty quick laps,

(*Drawing lines back and forth in the pool and then writing the number "40" over the lines.*)

careful to occasionally glance up at the very unathletic Stevens

(*Drawing a line from the pool to the "S."*)

who seemed oblivious to Ward, convincing Ward that Stevens wanted him to think he didn't suspect anything so he could trap Ward

(*Drawing a strong line from the "S" to the "W."*)

who wouldn't have any idea he was suspected. But Ward suspected everything,

(*Drawing huge circles, encompassing everything on the blackboard.*)

and when Honor didn't glance up at him once,

(*Drawing the number "1" on the right side of the blackboard.*)

he was sure he was right—

(*Directly to the audience.*)

or if he wasn't, that Honor was convinced he was.

3

(LEEDS *holds on the audience another moment, then turns his back on them.*)

BLACKOUT.

(*Out of darkness and silence there is the sound of a basket-ball being dribbled leisurely. The lights come up. Leeds is grading papers at his desk. From the cluttered desk he takes a pipe and lights it. The pipe is evidently not an instrument he uses to relax with, but a focus of energy, perhaps even a means of controlling his explosiveness. He wears a shirt now over the turtleneck and shoulder holster. Ward is dribbling the basketball; he is wearing a bathing suit which displays his body and sexual apparatus to best advantage; he is bull-ish. Ward casually hooks the ball into the basket, catching the ball as it skims the net. He fixes on Leeds. He is a man who works from hedged bets.*)

WARD: (*Dribbling the basketball near* LEEDS *to get his attention.*) You wanna make a bet, Leeds?

LEEDS: (*Without interest and without looking up.*) No.

WARD: How do you know?

LEEDS: I don't believe in betting.

WARD: This is an excellent bet. Don't you even wanna hear what it is?

(WARD *dribbles once, makes a casual head fake, and lays the the ball up and in.*)

LEEDS: (*Without interest.*) What is it?

WARD: (*Crossing back to* LEEDS.) I'm willing to bet you a hundred dollars that I can fuck Honor Stevens inside . . . what?—a month, three weeks. Name it. Make it tough, I need the work.

(LEEDS *is unresponsive.*)

Okay—make it two hundred that I can get her inside ten days.

(LEEDS *displays no interest.*)

4

Three hundred and inside a week.

(*Nothing from* LEEDS.)

Okay, my final offer, Leeds. Listening? Four hundred dollars and I get her inside five days. That's it. Take or leave it.

LEEDS: (*Without looking up.*) How about the divorcee downstairs?

WARD: That pig! Look, Leeds, it's got to be Honor Stevens. I've balled everybody in the building but her that I want to. Her number's come up and that's all there is to it.

LEEDS: Why don't you expand your operations to the building next door?

WARD: They've got a kidney shaped pool. I don't like kidney shaped pools. I mean, what *is* this sudden interest in Honor Stevens, Leeds? I don't get it.

LEEDS: (*Trying to end the conversation.*) If you get Honor Stevens, her husband *could* find out. If her husband *did* find out, they *might* get a divorce. If they *got* a divorce, I *probably* wouldn't have a ride to class at 7:30 every morning.

WARD: Why not?

LEEDS: Because *he* probably wouldn't take me anymore.

(WARD *makes a less casual drive on the basket.*)

WARD: Maybe she'd get the car.

LEEDS: She has ten o'clock classes.

WARD: (*Sitting at the counter.*) Look, Leeds, whudduya say we forego your eternal self-interests a minute and talk about the practical aspects of this thing.

LEEDS: (*Fixing on* WARD.) How can a mechanical penis taking a master's degree in physical education hope to talk about the practical aspects of anything?

WARD: By feeling like it.

LEEDS: I see.

5

WARD: (*Rising and shooting a casual basket.*) You know what your trouble is, Leeds?

LEEDS: Yes, I know what my trouble is.

WARD: You don't care about anything or anybody but yourself.

LEEDS: I see.

WARD: Yeah, you *do* see.

LEEDS: That's what I said.

WARD: I know.

LEEDS: But what you really mean is that I don't see.

WARD: That's right.

LEEDS: Which makes you wrong. Because I do see. But not what you think I think you think I see.

WARD: (*Crossing to* LEEDS.) *Look*—are you gonna offer some resistance and bet or not?

(LEEDS *seems totally uninterested.* WARD *swoops in on* LEEDS' *ear.*)

She can't stand you, Leeds. Think about that. Think about the way she's always tearin you to shreds. Think about what I'll do to her for you.

LEEDS: Why would I want to bet against you then?

WARD: Because I need the incentive, goddammit! I'm tired of balling all these chicks without any incentive!

(LEEDS *ignores him, rises and starts toward the bedroom.* WARD *backs off, turns suddenly and stops* LEEDS.)

How about a buck I get her by midnight?

LEEDS: Why not be done with it, Ward, and simply admit you want any justification you can come up with for wreaking havoc, creating misery, and indulging your psychopathic sexual appetite?

(LEEDS *disappears into bedroom.*)

6

WARD: (*Casually shooting basket.*) Justification! Of what? *For* what? Justify nothing to no one, Leeds. Just do!

LEEDS: (*Entering from bedroom engrossed in a book.*) You know, you're in the wrong game. You shouldn't be a phys. ed. teacher—uh-uh; you should have made a career of the army with the contingency they keep you a buck private forever.

WARD: Look who's belittling the army. The guy who wouldn't serve.

LEEDS: It's not that I wouldn't serve. It's that they wouldn't take me.

WARD: Oh yeah? Then what if they had taken you?

LEEDS: (*Focusing on* WARD.) I wouldn't have served. But that's not the point of this discussion, is it?

WARD: What *is* the point of this discussion, Leeds?

LEEDS: That there is none.

WARD: It's *my* discussion, I oughta know what the point is.

LEEDS: (*Crossing to desk and putting book down.*) Yes, but you don't. And to prove it, I am going to bet you not one, two, three, or four, but *five* hundred dollars that there is no point to your plot to seduce Honor Stevens. You have five seconds.

(LEEDS *unbares his watch.* WARD *confidently bounces his basketball.*)

WARD: The point to it, Leeds—the point to it is that I *want to do it.*

LEEDS: How do you know you want to do it? You have two seconds left.

WARD: (*Sitting in director's chair.*) I feel it!

LEEDS: (*Going to* WARD.) Wrong, and your time's up—sorry. We don't feel reasons, Ward.

WARD: No?

LEEDS: We think reasons.

7

WARD: Gee.

LEEDS: And in coming to conclusions—even "I want"—there has to be some mental justification process. If you cannot justify, simply mentally, how you know you want, you cannot know, to begin with, *that* you want and therefore cannot want.

(*Holding out a flat palm to* WARD.)

You owe me five hundred dollars. Pay up.

(WARD *slaps the basketball into* LEEDS' *palm and moves away into kitchen.*)

WARD: That's very interesting, Leeds.

LEEDS: (*Crossing to toy box and getting out a pump valve.*) I'm glad.

WARD: (*With his head in refrigerator.*) You are certainly an interesting person.

(LEEDS *inserts valve into basketball, crosses to spool table, and sits on basketball.* WARD *crosses toward bedroom, sees what* LEEDS *is doing, and goes to him.*)

That's my basketball, Leeds.

(LEEDS *stares at him. The air escapes.*)

LEEDS: (*Finally removing the valve.*) That *was* your basketball. It is now your deflated piece of rubber.

(LEEDS *dumps the basketball on the floor. It is dead.*)

WARD: (*Picking up ball.*) Well, you're takin it down to the gas station, goddammit, and gettin it blown back up.

LEEDS: Fine. And now that we've exchanged these little pleasantries, Ward, let's get down to it. I will bet you double or nothing on the five hundred you owe me that—

WARD: The five hundred I owe you . . .

LEEDS: Yes, Ward, the five hundred you owe me. And you either bet, pay up, or I'm going to murder you.

(LEEDS *stands and casually crosses his arms, one hand going unseen beneath his shirt to the shoulder holster.*)

8

So, what'll it be? Will you bet, will you pay up, or will you be murdered?

WARD: (*Jocularly defiant.*) Murdered.

(LEEDS *draws the revolver from beneath his shirt, checks the cylinder to be sure the bullet is in the right chamber, and aims at* WARD's *face.* WARD *snorts and turns and strolls toward his toy box.* LEEDS *alters his aim and fires at one of* WARD's *pictures, hitting it squarely between the eyes.* WARD *runs into the bedroom, slamming the door.*)

Leeds!

LEEDS: Hmm?

WARD: *Are you crazy? Wait! Are you waiting?*

LEEDS: Yes. Will you bet, pay up, or shall we see if a second shot can penetrate this cheap but fire resistant beaverboard?

WARD: Pay up! Lemme get my checkbook.

LEEDS: Cash.

WARD: *Cash?* It's eight o'clock at night. Where am I gonna get five hundred cash?

LEEDS: Nowhere. So we'll bet.

WARD: You don't believe in betting.

LEEDS: I don't believe in absolutes either.

WARD: (*Opening the bedroom door a crack and peeking out.*) Can I come out?

LEEDS: What do I care?

WARD: Uh, Leeds, how bout puttin the gun away?

LEEDS: It's empty.

WARD: Whudduya mean it's empty?

LEEDS: I only had one bullet.

WARD: Whudduya mean ya only had one bullet?

9

LEEDS: How many bullets does it take to kill someone?

WARD: (*Coming out of the bedroom. Compulsively defiant.*) Evidently more than one.

(LEEDS *suddenly points the gun at* WARD's *face again.* WARD *throws himself in terror against the wall.* LEEDS *pulls the trigger. The gun clicks, empty.*)

LEEDS: If I had wanted to kill you, Ward, you'd be dead; just as, if I ever *do* want to kill you, you *will* be dead.

WARD: I see, Leeds.

LEEDS: (*Indicating the hole in* WARD's *picture.*) I certainly hope so.

(*Crossing to his desk.*)

WARD: (*Spotting the damage.*) *Goddammit, Leeds, I don't have the negative to that one.*

(*His competitiveness coming to the fore. Crossing to* LEEDS.)

Okay. Okay, what's the bet—even though I *don't* owe you five hundred dollars?

LEEDS: (*Placing gun and holster in its hiding place on bookshelf.*) The wager is double or nothing on the five hundred. The structure of the competition is this: We are *both* betting that you can seduce Honor Stevens. However, if within forty-eight hours after you've first been to bed with her, her husband makes an attempt on your life or kills you, you lose. If he makes an attempt on your life or kills you *after* forty-eight hours, you win. Are you game?

WARD: (*Pause.*) Yeah!

(*They shake hands.* WARD *slams his basketball into his toy box and snatches up his football. He drops back to pass. Realizing what he has bet and crossing back to* LEEDS.)

No! Now look, Leeds, first of all I *don't* owe you five hundred dollars—

LEEDS: Oh yes you do.

WARD: —and second of all, I don't stand to win anything. That's not fair!

LEEDS: (*Sits.*) I don't believe in fair.

WARD: Well, then, it's not *right*, damn it. You *do* believe in right.

LEEDS: How the hell do you deduce that?

WARD: (*Cleverly.*) How *don't* you deduce it?

LEEDS: By not believing that right is in any even relatively absolute sense deducible.

WARD: Yeah? And how do you deduce *that*?

LEEDS: I don't, Ward. It's inductive by my disbelief in wrong.

WARD: Well, tough, because I wanna be able to win something.

(*He catches a picture of himself.*)

Christ, what am I arguing with you for? The bet's on, Leeds. You wanna think it's double or nothing on five hundred, have a nice time.

(WARD *gets down under an imaginary center with his football and barks signals.*)

Red, right, ninety-nine, set, *hut—*

(*He receives the snap and fades to pass, then runs through a broken field into the bedroom. There's a knock at the door.* WARD *peeks out of the bedroom.*)

Hey, you wanna grab that, Leeds?

LEEDS: No, I don't think so.

WARD: (*Running into kitchen, getting lazy susan of fruit, and placing it decoratively on counter.*) And after you grab it, how bout gettin outta here for a coupla hours?

LEEDS: Why? Who is it?

WARD: (*Handing* LEEDS *his jacket and the football.*) You know who it is, Leeds.

LEEDS: What's she doing here?

WARD: Well, she's here, Leeds, so that I can help her study for a calculus exam she has tomorrow.

LEEDS: What the hell do you know about calculus?

11

WARD: Nothin.

LEEDS: Very clever.

WARD: (*Straightening up spool table.*) Jesus, I really appreciate that, Leeds.

LEEDS: Very clever.

WARD: (*Crossing to counter, clearing trash from it, and opening bottle of* Airwick.) Repeating yourself isn't going to make things any easier for you. Now would you mind gettin the door and then gettin out?

(WARD *crosses to picture with bullet hole, rips it from wall, dumps it under couch, and moves another picture to cover hole in wall.*)

LEEDS: I have twenty-five freshman themes to grade before 10:30 tomorrow morning so that I may maintain my teaching assistantship. I have an examination at one for which I need lengthy preparation. So yes, I very definitely would mind getting out.

(*A second knock at the door, this one a bit irascible.*)

WARD: (*Calling.*) Be right there.

(WARD *whips quietly to the pile of Little League bats, selects a bat and taps the floor to get* LEEDS' *attention.* LEEDS *looks at him.* WARD *offers to choose* LEEDS *on the bat. After a moment,* LEEDS *nods and dumps his jacket and the football on his desk.* WARD *tosses him the bat and they choose,* WARD *employing a nice "chicken foot" maneuver along the way.* WARD *wins.*)

You lose, g'bye.

(*Runs to return bat to pile.*)

LEEDS: (*Crossing center.*) Three out of five.

WARD: No do-overs, Leeds, g'bye.

LEEDS: When I was interviewing roommates last year, Ward, I evidently failed to cover the subject of do-overs; however, now that it's arisen—

WARD: G'bye, Leeds.

LEEDS: Two out of three, just to be sporting—

WARD: No!

LEEDS: (*Returning to his desk.*) Then I'm not leaving.

(*A third knock at the door.*)

WARD: (*Rushing to* LEEDS *and pushing hard.*) You want me to screw her, don't ya?

LEEDS: Oh, nothing more.

WARD: Then go to your goddamn office.

LEEDS: Uh-uh. You wanted me to make it tough for you? Well, here's tough.

(LEEDS *smacks an additional pile of themes on the pile he's working on.*)

Come in.

(WARD *hurriedly exits to the bedroom. The front door opens and* HONOR STEVENS *stands there. She is a very attractive young woman in a simple, sophisticated way. She is not intimidated by* LEEDS, *although she is more flexible than he is, capable of being honest when he is not. At least until the second act their exchanges are head-on duels between nearly equal cynics. She carries several calculus books.*)

HONOR: (*Moving easily into the room.*) Good evening, John.

LEEDS: Honor.

HONOR: Sorry to have kept you waiting, John. Forgive me.

LEEDS: We'll see.

HONOR: (*Going to couch and putting books down.*) Bless you, John. I have an appointment with Ward. Is he here?

LEEDS: I didn't see you on his schedule for this evening.

HONOR: (*Turning to* LEEDS.) Well, I'm on it. I have something to take care of this evening, John, and I'd like you to get out of here, I'd really like you out of here.

13

LEEDS: Well, actually—

HONOR: And I don't have any time to waste on verbal gymnastics. Perhaps we can resume the competition later in the week.

LEEDS: (*Insisting on saying what he was going to say.*) Well, actually I'm rather deeply involved in several hundred freshman themes.

HONOR: You're not deeply involved in a goddamn thing. Now get the hell out of here.

(*Sits on couch.*)

(*A knock at the door. At the sound,* HONOR *turns away, seeming to know who's doing the knocking. Taking his lead from her,* LEEDS *speaks even as he opens the door.*)

LEEDS: Ah! . . . Stevens.

(RON STEVENS *is conservatively dressed, a young scientist without wit, but a very intelligent, very well educated man who is so nearly guileless that he is almost hopelessly vulnerable to the likes of* LEEDS, WARD, *and* HONOR. *He steps uneasily into the room, distracted from his purpose in coming and made even more uneasy by* LEEDS' *greeting to him. He is stuck between* LEEDS' *verbal barrage and the need to deal with his wife.*)

RON: (*Pausing at the front door.*) Did you call me Stevens, John?

LEEDS: Yes, I did.

RON: (*Nodding; then crossing to* HONOR.) Honor, may I see you outside?

HONOR: No.

LEEDS: (*Crossing to counter.* STEVENS *is now stuck between* HONOR *and* LEEDS.) And I wonder if you'd mind calling me Leeds.

RON: (*To* HONOR.) May I ask why?

LEEDS: Because my name is Leeds.

14

RON: (*To* LEEDS.) Yes, I'm well aware of that, John . . .

LEEDS: Leeds.

RON: (*Moving toward* LEEDS.) . . . but I've always called you John and you've called me Ron.

LEEDS: That was before.

RON: Before what?

LEEDS: Before I told you to call me Leeds. My name is Leeds.

RON: Yes, but your name is also John.

LEEDS: Yes, and in that case, it's also Leeds. So call me Leeds.

RON: All right, I'll play along. But you can still call me Ron.

LEEDS: Oh, no! Not if you're going to call me Leeds. I'll call you Stevens.

HONOR: You know, John, it's reassuring somehow to find someone as consistently tiresome as you. What else is new?

LEEDS: New? Well, this isn't exactly new, but I'm constipated.

(*Crossing to desk.*)

HONOR: Uhm.

LEEDS: And I am not enjoying a new pipe tobacco which tastes like lactic acid.

(*Sits at desk.*)

RON: (*Almost unconsciously spitting out the formula, then stuck with it.*) $CH_3CHOHCOOH$.

(LEEDS *stares at him.*)

Lactic acid.

(LEEDS *stares at him.*)

Not very good for constipation, I'm afraid.

(LEEDS *smiles a tight-lipped, unamused smile at him.*)

Might make you throw up though.

15

HONOR: It seems to me that for someone of John's general disposition, one orifice ought to be as good as another.

LEEDS: She's crazy about me. And it's important to me. I worry about what she thinks of me.

HONOR: Would you tell Ward I'm here?

LEEDS: Oh, I think he knows. Great intuition, that boy.

RON: (*Moving to* HONOR, *confidentially.*) Honor, I'd really like to talk to you a minute.

HONOR: Not now, Ronald.

(*The three of them stand in silence. Finally* RON, *made the most uncomfortable by the silence, has to break it.*)

RON: (*Crossing center. To* LEEDS.) I think we'll make it to school tomorrow morning. It was just the clutch cable. Needed a little tightening.

(*Nothing.*)

(*Toward* HONOR.)

I suppose we really ought to sell it. Get bikes like Ward.

(*Nothing.*)

Aw, I'll hang on to it for a while. Has a certain sentimental value. That V-Dub was the first thing Honor and I bought together.

WARD: (*Entering in a tennis outfit complete with sweat bands.*) Honor!

HONOR: Ward.

WARD: (*Crossing to* RON *and giving him a thorough handshake.*) Ron! What a nice surprise.

HONOR: Surprise?

LEEDS: Yes, Ward, what kind of surprise?

WARD: Well . . . that Ron is with you.

LEEDS: Ah! Yes, that *is* surprising. Stevens, why are you with me?

16

RON: I'm not. I'm with Honor.

LEEDS: Then no wonder Ward is surprised.

WARD: Who said he's with you?

LEEDS: You did. You said, "Well, that Ron is with you" after I—

WARD: I meant that Ron is with Honor.

LEEDS: Then why didn't you say so?

WARD: I did say so, Leeds.

LEEDS: (*Crossing between* WARD *and* RON.) Oh no you didn't. And we're not falling for the ole I-did-say-so-Leeds trick, either. Why shouldn't they be together?

WARD: Because I have to help Honor study for her calculus exam.

LEEDS: What the hell's that got to do with Stevens?

WARD: Nothing.

LEEDS: (*Fixing on* RON.) Then why are you here, Stevens?

RON: I . . . just stopped in to say that I'm going out for ice cream for everybody.

HONOR: (*The implication being that she'll hasten his exit.*) I'll get the bowls.

(*She exits to the kitchen.*)

(*The three men track her with their eyes.* WARD *moves to dart board and nervously throws a few.*)

LEEDS: (*Following* WARD.) There—you see how simple things are when you say what you mean so people can understand what you mean. Stevens is going out for ice cream for everybody and his wife is lining up bowls even as we speak. I think what each of us is wondering, Ward, is what contribution you're going to make to this evening's festivities.

WARD: (*Turning to* LEEDS.) Who said I wanted any ice cream?

LEEDS: Hmm—he may have you there, Stevens. You may be lying by promising to go out for ice cream for everybody.

17

(*To* WARD.)

Will you *eat* some of Stevens' ice cream?

RON: (*Joining* WARD *and* LEEDS.) I didn't say I was paying for all of it.

LEEDS: (*To* WARD.) Will you eat some of *the* ice cream?

WARD: What's the difference? You know what I mean, Leeds? I mean what's it got to *do* with anything?

LEEDS: Well, it's got everything to do with whether Stevens is going out for ice cream for everybody or not everybody.

WARD: Yeah, but who *cares?*

LEEDS: Well, evidently Stevens does, Ward; otherwise, he wouldn't be here, would he? Have a little respect for the commitments of others.

HONOR: (*Who has entered during this last line with bowls and spoons. Sitting in armchair.*) Speaking of the commitments of others, John, I wonder if you'd mind respecting the one I have to my exam tomorrow.

LEEDS: Not a chance.

HONOR: (*To* WARD.) Would you mind saying you'll have some ice cream so that we can get on with this?

WARD: Yeah . . . okay, I'll have some.

RON: Fine.

LEEDS: Well, now that that's settled it's—

HONOR: Now that that's settled, Ron will go out for the ice cream, Ward will help me with my calculus, and you'll do whatever you do when no one will listen to you.

LEEDS: (*Sitting in director's chair.*) No . . . now that Ward has agreed to eat some of the ice cream, it's safe to say that Stevens is indeed going out for ice cream for everybody— insofar, of course, as everybody here can be construed not to mean everybody everywhere. Now, as to financial respon- sibility—

18

HONOR: I'll pay for it—how's that?

RON: (*Crossing above* HONOR.) If you pay for it, though, that means I'm paying for it.

WARD: Jesus, *I'll* pay for it!

RON: Well, if you're paying for it, then why don't you go get it? I've lost interest.

LEEDS: (*To* RON.) Because then you wouldn't be going out for ice cream for everybody and that's why you . . . stopped in.

RON: (*Pause.*) I'm going out for ice cream for everybody.

(RON *starts to front door.*)

WARD: Hey, why don't you take Leeds with you?

LEEDS: With my knees? Are you crazy?

RON: (*To* WARD.) I can assure you I don't need anybody to go with me.

LEEDS: Stevens, we're talking at cross purposes here. None of us questions, I'm sure, whether or not you're capable of going out by yourself for ice cream for everybody, but whether—

RON: *Okay!* Gee God, so go with me already. Let's go. Okay?

LEEDS: (*Recognizing, if reluctantly, that it's time to be getting on with it.*) Okay.

(WARD *moves to front door to usher them out.*)

RON: Okay.

(RON *exits.* LEEDS *moves unhurriedly to exit, stops.*)

LEEDS: (*To* WARD *and* HONOR, *as permission.*) Okay.

(*He exits.*)

(WARD, *of course, plans now to put the "make" on* HONOR; *but, in point of fact,* HONOR *is simply going to use* WARD *to get rid of her husband by the cruellest means possible. Whereas* WARD *thinks he's seducing the hell out of her in this scene, she's in complete control and playing him for a fool.*)

19

WARD: Thought they'd never leave.

(*She is blank.* WARD *moves to her, touches her hair, moves it from her neck, and then kisses her neck. Suddenly the door opens and* LEEDS *leans in.*)

LEEDS: Hey, we forgot to decide on flavors. . . . Oh well, hell, don't worry about it. We'll manage.

(*He exits.*)

WARD: (*Pause. He turns his attention back to* HONOR, *snorts, throws an amused thumb after* LEEDS. *She doesn't seem amused. He tries to pick up his rhythm. Emotionlessly she denies his advance by rising and crossing to the couch. Pause.*) What's the deal?

HONOR: Is there a deal?

WARD: Well, down at the pool there sure seemed to be.

HONOR: Don't rush me, Ward.

WARD: (*Crossing to* HONOR *at couch.*) Listen, take all the time you want.

(*She has taken a cigarette from her purse and crosses to counter, sitting on a bar stool. She holds cigarette and matches, indicating she would like her cigarette lighted.* WARD *follows her to counter and gazes for a moment into her eyes before he notices the cigarette.*)

Here, lemme get that for you.

(*He lights her cigarette.*)

HONOR: You're so gallant, Ward.

(WARD, *a nonsmoker, reacts to the prospect of what her breath is going to smell like and lifts the lid from a candy dish on the spool table.*)

WARD: *Clorets.* And three different flavors of *Certs.* I'm outta wintergreen.

(*Seductively.*)

Want one?

HONOR: Not just yet.

WARD: No hurry, Honor, no hurry.

(WARD *wanders a little, trying to appear as if there's no hurry but doing a mediocre job of it.*)

Just . . . do what you *feel*, Honor.

HONOR: I am.

WARD: (*Swooping in on her.*) What for? Hell, that's your trouble, let yourself go. . . . Oh, I know, you're worried about getting hurt.

HONOR: Am I?

WARD: Sure!

(*Pause.*)

Aren't you?

HONOR: Let's say for the sake of argument that I am. What do you say next?

WARD: (*Moving away dramatically.*) I say, Who *hasn't* been hurt?

HONOR: Ron.

WARD: (*Aggressively.*) Everybody should be hurt. Hurt plus joy divided by ex equals life, Honor. The unhurt are the unborn . . . "I wept the day I was born and each day shows me why."

(*Moving in on her again.*)

Honor, let me be honest with you. I think I'm . . . falling in love with you.

HONOR: Falling in love? . . . Have you ever wondered, Ward, why we *fall* in love? Why always that sense of entrapment and doom? . . . Why don't we ever *rise* in love?

WARD: (*Pause.*) I think, then, that I'm . . . rising in love with you.

HONOR: That's . . . that's beautiful, Ward.

WARD: Well, it may not be beautiful, but I mean it from my heart.

HONOR: That's another image I adore.

WARD: (*Pressing on.*) What do you feel for me, Honor?

HONOR: Contempt.

WARD: (*Laughing it off.*) All kidding aside—

HONOR: (*Moving away from* WARD *to* LEEDS' *desk.*) Who's kidding?

WARD: You are!

(*Pause. He presses, following her.*)

This may sound . . .

(*Can't find the right word.*)

. . . *some*thing, Honor—

HONOR: (*Moving away from* WARD *and crossing to his toy box.*) Sheer poetry, Ward—

WARD: (*Following.*) —but I feel that there's a . . . a line of communication between us that . . . Oh hell, look, Honor, why bullshit about it? I want to make love to you. I think that for the first time in my life I truly want to make love to someone.

HONOR: (*Turning to him.*) And you want me to make love to you in return.

WARD: No—it would be enough just for me—I mean, sure, it would be an added bonus but—

HONOR: Ron has wanted me to make love in return to him for five years.

WARD: Why haven't you?

HONOR: I don't love him.

WARD: Why not?

HONOR: Why would I? How could I? Why should I?

22

WARD: Why the hell did ya marry him?

HONOR: (*Moving away from* WARD *and crossing back to* LEEDS'
          desk. For herself rather than WARD.) I married him because
          I was eighteen and because he was there; because I wanted
          to go away from where I was and he was going somewhere.

WARD: (*Following, but at a distance.*) Where?

HONOR: Nowhere, as it's turned out. I think he envisions us end-
          ing up on some quaint little campus somewhere where he'll
          discover the cure for all the afflictions of mankind . . . and
          where I will go quietly out of my only mind.

WARD: Uh-huh, uh-huh . . .

HONOR: (*With bitter ironic humor.*) You know, Ward, it's hu-
          morous, but I've just come in the last several months to a
          momentous realization which has become the source of some
          incredibly unhumorous disagreement between my husband
          and me and my father and me, but which someone as sensi-
          tive as you will certainly appreciate.

WARD: (*Disinterested and acutely aware that* RON *and* LEEDS
          will be back shortly.) Oh yeah?

HONOR: Am I boring you?

WARD: No, no, certainly not. What'd ya realize?

HONOR: That my life mustn't be pledged to anything or any-
          body against my will if I can do anything to prevent it.

WARD: Uh-huh. Very good.

HONOR: This is my only life.

WARD: That's very good.

HONOR: There are no seconds and no rewards. So what do you
          suppose I did this morning?

WARD: About what?

HONOR: (*Crossing to couch.*) I told him that I've decided not
          to finish my masters just now and that if and when I do de-
          cide to finish it, it won't be in elementary education, be-
          cause—

23

(*To* WARD.)

as I'm sure you've been tempted to tell me many times—
I've never wanted to be an . . . elementary . . . school . . .
teacher. So I'm not going to be.

WARD: Very smart.

HONOR: I told him I'm going to leave school altogether at the
end of this quarter and I'm going to get some kind of job and
I'm going to think. About myself.

WARD: (*Moving to her. Seductively.*) Why don't ya divorce
him?

HONOR: (*Returning from a mental distance to the sheer reality
of* WARD.) Because two weeks ago when I suggested a divorce . . .

(*Putting the onus on* WARD.)

. . . he threatened various forms of radical behavior.

WARD: You didn't believe him, did you?

HONOR: Actually, Ward, I didn't give it a whole lot of thought
either way.

WARD: My point exactly. . . . Come to bed with me.

HONOR: All right, Ward.

WARD: You will? What if they catch us?

HONOR: I guess that's a chance we'll have to take.

(*She exits to the bedroom.*)

WARD: (*At the bedroom door.*) Honor . . . come to bed. Come
share my bed, come . . . share my life.

(WARD *stares after her a moment, then swings into action.
He puts the chain lock on the door and grabs a breath mint
and pops it into his mouth as he exits after her.*)

BLACKOUT.

Lights up.

(WARD *enters adjusting his sweat bands.*)

Okay. Let's move 'em out. Hey-yup!

(*He crosses to front door and unlocks it, then he goes to his toy box and takes a very thick notebook out. He sits on the director's chair and turns well past the middle of the notebook. He begins to check off and write the particulars called for.*)

Honor Stevens . . . Caucasian . . . Married . . . Volkswagen . . .

(*Calling toward the bedroom.*)

Hey, how old are you?

HONOR: (*Soberly.*) Twenty-three. Why?

WARD: (*To himself absently.*) Why what? . . .

(*Writes her age.*)

Student . . . Total expenditure?

(*Thinks a moment and then with a certain pride.*)

None.

(*He stares toward the bedroom, evaluating her.*)

About a C-minus . . .

(*Double-checks his appraisal.*)

Yeah—a C-minus.

(*He begins to write his remarks as* HONOR *enters. She stands emotionlessly in the doorway a moment and then says intuitively.*)

HONOR: What's that?

WARD: This? This is my notebook.

HONOR: It's some sort of rating sheet, isn't it?

WARD: A what? A rating sheet! Now what would I be doing with a— Yeah, it's a rating sheet, so what?

HONOR: (*Crossing to above* WARD.) I suppose I ought to ask you what you gave me.

WARD: Well, there's no rule against asking—

HONOR: What did you give me?

WARD: —but there is a rule against telling. I can send you a report card in the mail with a grade and some criticisms following each of our . . . uh—

HONOR: Fucks.

WARD: No, each of our—

HONOR: Screws, bangs—

WARD: No—

HONOR: balls—

WARD: No—

HONOR: boffs—

WARD: No—

HONOR: planks, lays—

WARD: No—

HONOR: plugs, pokes—

WARD: Each of our—sessions of . . . *love*-making.

HONOR: Perhaps at this time, Ward, I ought to explain to you what actually happened between us this evening.

WARD: (*Crossing to the toy box to replace the notebook.*) What for?

HONOR: (*Laughing sardonically.*) Forgive me. I lost my head there for a moment.

WARD: You wanna siddown a minute while I figure out the batting averages for my Little League team?

HONOR: (*Sitting in director's chair.*) Absolutely.

(*She laughs again.* WARD *dumps his notebook into his toy box and brings out his Little League log book.* LEEDS *enters.*)

(LEEDS *is obviously not in the best of spirits, but* RON *has evidently asked him to give him a big intro.* LEEDS *looks across* HONOR *and* WARD, *then gestures less than enthusiastically to the door.*)

LEEDS: The ice cream man cometh.

(RON *leaps through the door past* LEEDS *brandishing a three-gallon barrel of ice cream.*)

RON: *Ta-da!*

WARD: Jesus, what took ya so long? I didn't think I was gonna be able to hold out.

LEEDS: (*Closing the door. Dourly.*) Little car trouble.

RON: Not really, John.

LEEDS: Leeds.

RON: Every place was closed—that was really the trouble.

LEEDS: (*Crossing to counter.*) Couldn't get outa first gear there for a while—really touch and go.

RON: We had to finally convince a restaurant to sell us this whole thing.

LEEDS: They didn't have an insulated bag, it's melting.

(*Pause.* RON *crosses into kitchen, putting ice cream on counter.*)

How's the calculus coming?

(LEEDS *crosses to desk.*)

WARD: (*Snapping shut his Little League book and replacing it.*) Just finished.

HONOR: What flavor did you get?

RON: (*Moving to* HONOR. *Trying to make it fun for her.*) Guess.

HONOR: (*Rhetorically.*) Guess. . . . Butter pecan.

RON: Uh-uh.

HONOR: I give up.

27

RON: No—guess.

HONOR: Peppermint stick.

RON: Nooo.

HONOR: Neapolitan.

RON: Not quite. What's your favorite?

HONOR: My favorite . . . Mocha chip?

RON: Nooo—

WARD: How bout plain vanilla?

RON: Who says?

WARD: How bout French vanilla?

(RON *turns away, morosely agitated.*)

HONOR: You said my favorite. I'm sorry.

LEEDS: He asked what your favorite is. He didn't say he got it.
Could've just been a pop quiz.

RON: (*Trying for a late inning save of a lost ball game.*) That's
all they'd sell us. And Leeds had to explain to the kid very
carefully why he should sell us anything at all before he'd
even sell us French vanilla.

HONOR: I'll bet that was good.

RON: It was.

WARD: Why don't you tell us about it.

HONOR: Oh yes—by all means.

RON: (*For her.*) Should we?

HONOR: Sure.

RON: Okay!

WARD: God, is this gonna be a treat!

RON: (*Taking charge excitedly.*) I'll be you, Leeds, and you
be the kid.

LEEDS: Why can't I be me?

HONOR: Come on, John, give someone else a chance.

WARD: Frankly, I'm sick of you in the part.

LEEDS: (*Crossing into kitchen behind counter.*) You really know how to hurt a person.

WARD: (*Proudly.*) I know.

(*Moves armchair into good viewing position and helps* HONOR *into it. Then he moves director's chair very close to* HONOR.)

RON: Okay, we—

WARD: Wait a second. Gotta organize. Popcorn.

(WARD *grabs up his briefcase from beside toy box, a little kid's briefcase—and pulls from it a handful of popcorn. To* HONOR.)

I made it for class this morning but I didn't finish it. It's still fresh.

LEEDS: I had some for breakfast.

WARD: (*Sitting in director's chair beside* HONOR.) I make it with olive oil and garlic salt.

LEEDS: I think you'll find it has a consistency reminiscent of ear wax.

(*In the scene,* RON *does his damnedest to imitate* LEEDS. *Since* LEEDS *can't play the major role of himself in the scene, he competes with himself by padding the role of the kid.*)

(RON *takes up a banana from bowl of fruit on the breakfast bar and will use it for the gun.*)

RON: Okay, we come up to the counter of this restaurant, see, and Leeds says to the kid, he says . . .

(*Sticking the banana in the kid's face.*)

"You better have ice cream, kid, or I'm gonna kill you, and I mean it."

LEEDS: (*As stereotype gay.*) Well, of course we have ice cream, precious.

(LEEDS *kisses the tip of the banana.* RON *thrusts the banana down on the breakfast bar.*)

RON: Come on, Leeds!

LEEDS: You're Leeds, I'm the kid.

RON: I know that. Just cut it out; come on.

(LEEDS *straightens himself into a mock "good little boy" posture.*)

"You better have ice cream, kid, or I'm gonna kill you, and I mean it."

LEEDS: (*As the kid.*) "Heh heh. We got it."

RON: "Okay, okay, give us a quart of— What've you got?"

LEEDS: "Cones."

RON: "Whudduya mean, *cones?* That's not a flavor, you moron, that's a . . . that's a . . . *cone.*"

WARD: Excellent choice of a synonym, Leeds.

LEEDS: "All's we got, mister, is cones."

RON: (*Grabbing the kid by the cheeks and pulling his face to where they almost touch nose to nose.*) "What flavors?"

LEEDS: (*Reeling backwards from the "smell."*) Ptooey! Geez, you oughta quit smokin, mister, your breath smells pukey.

RON: "*What flavors?*"

LEEDS: Chocolate sidewalk, rump roast, and charcoal briquet.

RON: Come on!

LEEDS: (*Coming back to* RON *with mock seriousness.*) "Chocolate, strawberry, and vanilla."

(*Haughtily.*)

"French vanilla."

RON: (*Pointing to* WARD.) "What'll it be, Stevens?"

WARD: Rump roast sounds like a gas. Give us a side.

RON: (*Losing patience with the flow of the battle.*) So Stevens says, "Give us a quart of chocolate."

LEEDS: "Sorry, fella, can't spare it."

RON: So Stevens says—

WARD: "Make it a quart of strawberry."

LEEDS: (*To* WARD.) "No can spare."

RON: So Leeds says to Stevens, "Well, I guess that leaves French vanilla."

WARD: And Stevens says, boy, Leeds, you sure got a head on your shoulders, boy—

RON: (*Controlling himself.*) So Leeds says, "Give us a quart of French vanilla."

LEEDS: "Cones."

RON: "Okay, you son of a . . ."

(*He is reluctant to say "bitch" in front of* HONOR.)

LEEDS: "Geez, c'mon, mister. I said cones, didn't I? We got no containers, we got no bowls—we don't sell it no other way but by the cone. Gimme a break, mister . . . I just put a lotta bread in a used Yamaha." Aha . . . Ah-ho . . . shuffle off to Buffalo—

RON: *All right, hold it!*

(*Everyone holds it. Indicating the three-gallon container.* To WARD.)

"How much ice cream in that three-gallon container, Stevens?"

WARD: And Stevens says, three gallons!

RON: No! Stevens says, "I'd say approximately two and a half gallons."

LEEDS: "Oh, I'd say about—*Jesus*, the chubby guy's right!"

31

RON: (*To* WARD.) "Okay, we'll take it. Wrap the . . . blankety-blank thing up."

LEEDS: "Cones!"

RON: (*To* WARD.) "How many cones in two and a half gallons, Stevens?"

WARD: Uhm, lemme see, ex equals—

RON: (*Proudly.*) And quicker than a flash Stevens says, "I'd say about eighty-seven cones,"

(*To* LEEDS.)

and Leeds says to the kid, "Give us eighty-seven cones."

LEEDS: (*Starting to pull away.*) "Eighty-seven cones comin up!"

RON: "Except for one thing."

LEEDS: "What's that, mister?"

RON: "Don't put the ice cream in the cones."

LEEDS: (*Suspiciously.*) "I don't get it."

RON: "Put it in one of those empty three-gallon containers over there!"

(RON *turns to* HONOR *in triumph.*)

LEEDS: "What should I do with the cones?"

RON: (*Pause. He glances at* HONOR, *then leaps to the kid's ear and screams.*) "Stick 'em up your ass!"

(*Silence.*)

WARD: Stick 'em up your ass? You're going for a Ph.D. in English, Leeds? Stick 'em up your ass. That's terrific.

LEEDS: Men's room. Graduate school library. Third floor.

WARD: (*Returning director's chair to its place and sitting on couch.*) Stick 'em up your ass . . . God, what a story.

(*Silence.*)

LEEDS: The ice cream continues to melt.

(LEEDS *dishes up the ice cream, which by now is a very soupy confection.* RON *moves away from the breakfast bar— uneasy again—and stands beside* HONOR. *Discomfort. Finally, when something* has *to be said.*)

RON: (*To* HONOR.) You should've seen that kid. Boy, was he surprised when I told him how many cones there are in two and a half gallons of ice cream.

HONOR: (*Rising.*) I'll bet.

RON: Shocked is more like it.

(*Nothing. Returning her chair to its place.*)

You know, the funny thing is . . . vanilla really was your favorite.

HONOR: Was it?

RON: And I'll tell you how I know.

HONOR: (*More to herself. Crossing to director's chair and sitting.*) Whoever heard of someone forgetting her favorite ice cream?

RON: (*Following* HONOR.) The day we bought the V-Dub, we wanted to drive someplace special, so I said, why don't we drive out . . . you know— What was the name of that drive-in you kids used to sit around all the time when you were in high school?

HONOR: Coffee. That was my favorite.

RON: Coffee? Are you kidding me? Will you please try to remember the name of that drive-in back home where all you kids—

HONOR: Topper's.

RON: Roy's! It was Roy's.

HONOR: It wasn't Roy's.

RON: So we decided to drive out to Roy's—just for the heck of it—to have a root beer float. But you were afraid that a six-year-old car with fifty thousand miles on it wouldn't make it out to Roy's, so why didn't we just go across the street

33

from the car lot to this drug store and have an ice cream cone. And I said, probably all they've got is chocolate, strawberry, and vanilla. And you said, that's all right because vanilla was really your favorite anyway. You remember that.

HONOR: That doesn't sound like something I'd say.

RON: I'm tellin ya—vanilla, Honor!

(*Pause. She looks up at him, responds simply to this desperation.*)

HONOR: Maybe you're right.

LEEDS: (*Who has been watching the end of this little scene.*) Ice cream for everybody!

(LEEDS *takes his ice cream and goes to his desk.* WARD *goes to the kitchen and gets a bowl for himself and one for* HONOR, *then sits on the couch.* RON *gets himself a bowl and sits in the armchair.* LEEDS *and* WARD *take a slurping mouthful of the soupy stuff.* HONOR *eats . . . and finally* RON *eats, having tried to remain as stoic and cool in the face of the slurping as possible. As* RON's *spoon touches his lips,* LEEDS *and* WARD *simultaneously do a big:*)

LEEDS and WARD: *Yummy!*

RON: Is it all right?

(*Simultaneously.*)

LEEDS: *Yech!*   WARD: *Blah!*

RON: Don't you like it really?

LEEDS: *Terrific!*   WARD: *Great!*

RON: Is it?

LEEDS: *Blah!*   WARD: *Yech!*

HONOR: (*Amused in her unamused way.*) Oh, all right, stop it. It's fine, Ron.

WARD: Sure it's *fine*, Ron. Isn't it, Leeds?

34

LEEDS: Fine? Well, I don't— Fine . . . That's the word you're pushing?

(*Rolls it around.*)

Fine . . . Fine . . .

WARD: That's it on the nose, wouldn't you say?

LEEDS: No.

WARD: What?

LEEDS: Adequate. It's adequate—

WARD: Adequate!

LEEDS: —soup.

WARD: Ah! Adequate soup. You've pinpointed it!

LEEDS: Yes, it's adequate soup—

WARD: But—

LEEDS: —but lousy ice cream.

WARD: (*Just a beat behind* LEEDS.) —lousy ice cream. You're right, Leeds. I hate to admit it, but you really hit it that time.

HONOR: (*To* RON.) Eat your ice cream. They're just having fun with you.

LEEDS: (*Leaping on the word.*) Fun! You think *that* was fun? Wait till you see . . . *Ward's basketball scrapbook!* Where's your basketball scrapbook?

WARD: Ach. I lent it to somebody.

HONOR: You never told us you were a basketball star, Ward.

LEEDS: *Star?* Why I tell you this kid was so good that he had—I don't know *how* many colleges offered him scholarships. How many?

WARD: (*Modestly.*) Three.

LEEDS: (*Ed Sullivan wringing applause for a bad dog act.*) *How bout that!*

35

RON: That's not so many.

LEEDS: (*Playing right over* RON.) Pounding on his door. Offering him faculty wives, crates of oranges . . . jock straps.

(*Pause, suddenly remembering the topper.*)

A convertible. Hear this! Tell him about the school that offered you a convertible if you'd come play bouncy-ball for them.

WARD: Yeah, I was down at—

LEEDS: *How bout that!*

RON: I had twelve scholarship offers.

(*All turn on* RON. *Silence.*)

HONOR: (*Sardonically.*) Values, darling, values. Yours were academic. Ward's were athletic.

RON: So what?

LEEDS: (*The kid who starts fights between other kids and then stands back and enjoys watching them tear each other up.*) "So what?" Did you hear that, Ward? Stevens said, "So what?"

WARD: Yeah, I heard him. What's that supposed to mean: "So what?"

LEEDS: Obviously it means so what's the big deal about three lousy athletic scholarships when he got twelve academic scholarships.

RON: Half the morons in the world can get an athletic scholarship.

LEEDS: Maybe even more than half.

WARD: Oh, is that so—

RON: And they didn't offer me a convertible. Uh-uh, oh no. No sir! You know what they offered me?

LEEDS: A set of oxen?

RON: Tuition, room, and board. They didn't even pay my lab fees. You think lab fees are cheap?

WARD: Listen, you're talking to a guy who took zoology.

LEEDS: Three times.

WARD: Twice!

RON: Well, believe me lab fees aren't cheap!

WARD: Listen—don't tell me. I hadda buy my own frogs.

RON: Oh no you didn't! And you didn't have to pay for your meals in the cafeteria either.

WARD: I had to eat, didn't I?

RON: So did I! But I had to pay for my meals out of my scholarship money. They didn't have a special section of the cafeteria where I could eat steak—for *free*. They didn't even have a special section where I could eat steak if I paid for it. You know why?

WARD: Why?

RON: Because they didn't serve steak in our lousy section of the lousy cafeteria. And even if they did, I couldn't have afforded it on my lousy academic scholarship.

WARD: Keep talkin. I think I'm startin to get the picture.

RON: You know what I subsisted on for four years? Meat loaf and succotash! Do you know how many different ways those people found to make meat loaf and succotash during those four years?

WARD: How many?

RON: *One!*

WARD: (*Rising and crossing to counter to put bowl down.*) Meat loaf and succotash, huh? Okay, I got the picture. Okay. Okay . . . let's see ya stop me from scoring.

(WARD *yanks* RON *from the armchair.* WARD *clears all furniture from the center of the room.* HONOR *moves to couch.*)

Come on—let's see ya stop me from scoring.

RON: What do you mean?

37

WARD: Scoring! Scoring! Stop me from scoring.

RON: Here?

WARD: (*Crossing to toy box. Picking up and disgustedly discarding his deflated basketball.*) Yeah, here. You and me. One on one.

RON: We don't have a ball.

(LEEDS *indicates playing with an imaginary ball.*)

I mean—what's this got to do with—

WARD: Well, look, if you wanna chicken out, just say so.

RON: What's this got—what'll it prove?

WARD: Plenty.

(WARD *tosses* LEEDS *a referee's whistle.*)

Okay, ya ready?

(RON, *as he has done previously in the scene no doubt, looks to* HONOR *for a sign.*)

LEEDS: Go ahead, it'll be fun. Afterward you can quiz him in microbiology.

RON: (*Crossing to* WARD. *Pause; then putting down his bowl of ice cream and removing his jacket and giving it to* HONOR.)

All right . . . what exactly do I do?

WARD: Try and stop me.

(LEEDS *blows the referee's whistle and throws the imaginary ball up to begin the game. He takes a ready stance to catch any infractions of the rules.* WARD *dribbles the imaginary ball back toward* LEEDS' *desk.* RON *stares at him.* WARD *urges* RON *to try to steal the ball.* RON *lunges toward the ball and* WARD *dribbles the ball behind his back and to the other hand.* RON *lunges toward the ball again, and again* WARD *dribbles behind his back and switches hands.* RON *lunges a third time and* WARD *dribbles around him and drives in for an easy lay-up.*)

Swish!

LEEDS: Damn nice shot!

WARD: Two-nothing.

RON: Wait a minute! How do I know he made it?

WARD: Your ball.

(RON *just barely glances back at* WARD, *who passes him the ball.*)

RON: (*Taking another step toward* LEEDS.) How do I know—

(LEEDS *blows the whistle and he and* WARD *make the "walking" sign.*)

LEEDS: Walking with the ball!

WARD: My ball.

(WARD *grabs the ball from* RON *and goes around him for the easy score.*)

Swish! Four-nothing.

LEEDS: (*Announcing into the whistle.*) If you've just joined us, fans, it's four-nothing and young Ron Stevens is in big trouble. The youngster from next door just can't seem to get his offense rolling.

RON: (*Crossing to* LEEDS' *desk.*) Okay—gimme the ball!

(WARD *baby-tosses the ball to* RON, *who backs up and begins to dribble in his unathletic way.* RON *motions to* WARD *to come toward him.* WARD, *standing between* RON *and the basket, motions for* RON *to come toward him.* RON *dribbles madly toward the basket. As he passes* WARD, WARD *effortlessly reaches out his hand, and steals the ball.* RON *stops under the basket and looks back at* WARD. *Both of them stand dribbling and staring at each other.*)

WARD: I stole it.

RON: *Who says?*

LEEDS: He did, Stevens. I was just commenting to all the fans out there in tv land that that was a *honey* of a steal.

(WARD *fires a long jump shot over* RON.)

39

WARD: Swish! Six-nothing.

RON: Hold it! I wasn't ready.

WARD: You didn't call time. Six-nothing.

RON: Okay—I *quit.*

WARD: Quitter!

WARD and LEEDS: Stevens is a quitter, Stevens is a quitter!

(RON *backs up again to* LEEDS' *desk and dribbles wildly toward* WARD *and the basket. They collide, obviously because* WARD *moved into* RON's *path.* LEEDS *gives a blast of the whistle and he and* WARD *deliver the charging signal.*)

LEEDS: Charging on you, Stevens!

RON: (*Sprawled under the basket.*) Oh no you don't. I know the rules. He tripped me.

WARD: (*The innocent.*) I didn't budge.

RON: *Like fish you didn't!*

(WARD *flashes the "T"—for "technical foul"—sign at* LEEDS *who is in the process of calling the technical and delivering the sign himself at the same moment* WARD *calls for it.* HONOR *has begun to laugh lustily.*)

LEEDS: Okay—technical foul on you, Stevens!

RON: *What for?*

LEEDS: For saying, "Like fish."

RON: *Quit cheating! If you're going to play something—*

(WARD *and* LEEDS *are of the same mind again and both deliver the thumb.*)

LEEDS: Okay, you're *outta* the game, Stevens!

RON: *I quit!*

WARD: It's too late—Leeds already threw ya out.

RON: (*Turning on* HONOR, *who's laughing so hard she's nearly crying.*) It's pretty funny, isn't it, Honor? Boy.

(*A spoken laugh; two separate words.*)

Ha ha! Thanks a lot. I'm going.

(RON *snatches his jacket up and exits.* HONOR *begins to rein in her laughter.*)

WARD: (*Crossing to* LEEDS *and taking back the whistle.*) Christ, did you see him, Leeds? Absolutely no moves at all to his left.

LEEDS: (*Going back to his desk.*) Nice going, big guy. Just like the year you made All American. Tell Honor about the year you made All American.

(WARD *glances at* LEEDS *to see if* LEEDS *will permit him to heave a little bullshit.*)

WARD: (*Crossing to* HONOR *at couch.*) Yeah, well I made a few of—

LEEDS: Liar.

WARD: (*To* LEEDS.) Oh yeah?

LEEDS: Ward just didn't have it. The first time one of those big boys whacked him in the nose on a rebound, old Ward boy, he just packed it up. So long bouncy-ball.

WARD: Get off it, will ya!

(*To* HONOR.)

He doesn't know. I just decided since I was goin into coaching I'd better concentrate on—

LEEDS: —on bullshit.

WARD: I oughta know, *Leeds.*

LEEDS: And I'm sure you do, *Ward.* You didn't want to get marked up. You saw you didn't have it, so rather than chance jeopardizing your major industry, you—

WARD: *So what?*

LEEDS: So that was laudably realistic of you.

WARD: Yeah, but so what?

HONOR: Ron was Phi Beta Kappa.

WARD: (*To* HONOR.) What the hell's that got to do with anything?

HONOR: Oh, I don't know; just that he achieved the highest honor in his field and you evidently failed miserably at more than one—

WARD: I got "Best Looking" in the yearbook.

HONOR: Ron got "Most Intelligent" in his.

LEEDS: And you, of course, got "Most Likely to Succeed" in yours.

HONOR: Yes. That's right.

LEEDS: At what?

HONOR: There were no specifications.

LEEDS: How're ya doin?

HONOR: I'm sorting out my options.

LEEDS: Ah, so that's what you're doing.

WARD: (*Trying to turn the attention back to him and get this thing straightened out; indicating his frat picture on the wall.*) I was the first freshman ever elected social chairman of our fraternity.

HONOR: (*Looking past* WARD *to* LEEDS. *A fitting topper.*) Ron fixed our first apartment so that I could turn on the stove by pressing a button under my pillow.

WARD: Oh, yeah, well I once scored forty points in—

LEEDS: But Ward can swim the length of the pool six times. *Underwater.*

WARD: Six and a half. I broke my record Sunday.

LEEDS: You didn't tell me. Thanks a lot.

WARD: I don't have to tell you everything, Leeds.

LEEDS: Yeah, but something like that: Wow.

HONOR: I would just as soon the two of you didn't tease Ron like that. He's very sensitive to that sort of thing.

LEEDS: Let me hasten to note that you, among the three of us, are certainly to be commended as being most sympathetic to his sensitivity.

HONOR: I can assure you I don't need you to point out my insensitivity to me.

LEEDS: That's all right. No charge.

WARD: Hey, look, you don't have to feel guilty.

HONOR: About what?

WARD: About . . . whatever.

HONOR: (*Rising and collecting her books and purse.*) Just mind your own damn business, both of you.

LEEDS: What makes you think this is none of my business?

HONOR: (*Crossing to front door. Pause; she fixes on him.*) What makes you think it is?

LEEDS: (*Breaking from her.*) I never answer rhetorical questions.

WARD: (*Simultaneous with* LEEDS' *line.*) He never answers rhetorical questions.

(LEEDS *sits at his desk and takes up a theme to grade.*)

HONOR: You'll pardon me for changing the subject, but in a perverse way, I've come to find it amusing that you are so frightened of me.

LEEDS: You're right, that is amusing.

HONOR: What would you say I wonder if one day, by prior agreement—we'd have to work through agents of course—we would walk stripped and unarmed into an empty room somewhere.

LEEDS: The stripped part has a certain appeal, but unarmed—never.

(*He shakes his head.* WARD *laughs.*)

HONOR: You're sure this is the way you want to play, John?

LEEDS: Oh, yes.

HONOR: Fine. Goodnight, Ward.

(*She exits.*)

(WARD *returns the furniture to its place.*)

LEEDS: (*Trying to seem disinterested.*) How's the wager stand?

WARD: I screwed her.

LEEDS: Big deal.

WARD: Look, I've had a little more experience with women than you have.

LEEDS: So have most ninth graders.

WARD: Yeah? And to what do you attribute your lack of experience?

LEEDS: Lack of success. . . . What the hell's this got to do with anything? How was she in bed?

WARD: (*Crossing into the bedroom.*) What the hell's that got to do with anything?

LEEDS: I'm thinking of writing your biography. How was she?

WARD: (*From the bedroom.*) I gave her a C-minus.

LEEDS: What's wrong with her?

WARD: (*Reappearing at the bedroom door.*) She just *lays* there.

LEEDS: Hmph.

WARD: But I guess they can't all be A's and B's.

LEEDS: No, I guess not.

(*Holding up a banana.*)

From all us guys, Ward, who have to take a steady diet of C-minuses, I want to present this token of our gratitude to

44

you for knocking off a C-minus now and then and saving us that little extra wear and tear on our bodies.

(LEEDS *allows the banana to droop impotently, then throws it to* WARD.)

WARD: (*Picking up the banana.*) You think you're very goddamn clever, don't you, Leeds?

LEEDS: Yes, I do, Ward, but *you* think I think I'm cleverer than you think I am, when in fact you think I'm cleverer than I am. And that's one of the reasons why I'm king and you clean the stables.

WARD: Oh, yeah? And that's why I got that notebook in there and you got your fist and a subscription to *Playboy*.

(LEEDS *is silenced, if momentarily.* WARD *sits in director's chair.*)

You just stick with those words, Leeds. Just stick with those words, kid.

(*Checking his watch.*)

Okay, it's ten o'clock. Record the deed at nine. That puts me a mere forty-seven hours from victory.

LEEDS: Not quite.

WARD: (*Smugly.*) Unless, of course, ole Ronny-boy makes an attempt on my life.

LEEDS: Or kills you, Ward. Or kills you.

WARD: (*Still snug as hell.*) Right. Gotcha, Leeds. I'll tell ya, Leeds, I'm gettin bored already. Let's double the wager and say I gotta get her again in the next forty-seven hours. Huh? How about that?

LEEDS: Not bad. What have I got to gain though?

WARD: (*Crossing to* LEEDS.) Another vicarious treat, Leeds.

LEEDS: Let's say beyond that.

WARD: There'll be twice as much chance that Ron'll murder me.

LEEDS: Fascinating logic.

WARD: Bet?

LEEDS: Why bother? Lousy C-minus.

WARD: Look, you wanna bet or not?

LEEDS: Certainly I want to bet.

WARD: Okay!

(WARD *snaps the banana in half in* LEEDS' *face.*)

BLACKOUT.

ACT TWO

The following afternoon.

LEEDS *enters through the front door, glances to the emptiness of the living room, then toward the bedroom door. He dumps his jacket on one of the bar stools and plunks down a pack of themes on the desk.*

WARD *peeks around the bedroom doorway and enters. He is in the process of undressing himself. He moves swiftly on* LEEDS.

WARD: What are you doing here?

LEEDS: I live here.

WARD: I mean, why aren't you in class?

LEEDS: I don't feel well.

WARD: What's the matter?

LEEDS: I don't feel well.

WARD: I mean specifically.

LEEDS: Specifically, Ward, I do not *feel* well.

WARD: How'd ya get home?

LEEDS: By hunchback.

WARD: Look, I know you don't feel well, but would you mind telling me how you got *home*.

LEEDS: Stevens drove me in his motor car.

WARD: (*More to himself.*) So he's home then.

LEEDS: (*Going into the kitchen.*) If that's meant to be an Aristotelian syllogism, it's fallacious.

WARD: (*In hot pursuit.*) Goddammit, is he home?

LEEDS: I don't know anybody named Izzy.

WARD: Ron, Leeds!

LEEDS: Ron Stevens, you mean? He's right next door. I don't know any Ron Leeds though.

WARD: Look, do ya mind, I haven't got time for games!

LEEDS: Well, look you too, if you think I'm enjoying this, you idiot, you're a moron.

WARD: Okay—when are you leaving?

LEEDS: Tomorrow! Today I'm going to be sick. Here!

(*He starts for the bedroom.*)

WARD: (*Cutting him off and trying to keep him from the bedroom.*) Come on, dammit, Leeds. I was just about to start the clinic. There's more involved here than just the wager. This woman needs my help.

LEEDS: You needn't burden yourself with any therapeutic obligations. Nice of you to be concerned though. To keep things in perspective, Ward, Stevens has twenty-seven and a half hours in which to make retribution for what you have as yet only partly accomplished.

(LEEDS *goes to the bedroom doorway, calls in.*)

Come out, come out, wherever you are.

WARD: Thanks a lot.

LEEDS: (*To* WARD. *Taking afghan from couch and sitting in armchair.*) You're very subtle. You'd be superb in the role of a panic-stricken crowd.

(HONOR *enters from the bedroom and stands coolly, calmly in the doorway.*)

LEEDS: Hello, Honor.

HONOR: John.

LEEDS: Honor.

HONOR: Yes?

LEEDS: Ron is home.

48

HONOR: Is he?

LEEDS: No. Ron.

WARD: (*Standing between* HONOR *and* LEEDS.) Stay out of this, will ya!

(*To* HONOR.)

Honor, now listen to me—

HONOR: I'm going to talk to John now, Ward.

WARD: Later. Ron's home.

HONOR: Yes, I know—John just told me. Did I hear you say you aren't feeling well, John?

LEEDS: I don't know, did you?

HONOR: (*Crosses to spool table opposite* LEEDS.) Perhaps I could diagnose your problem. Do you hate me, John?

LEEDS: No—you hate you, Honor.

WARD: What are you asking him that for?

LEEDS: (*To* HONOR.) I don't hate you. I don't care enough about you to hate you. I don't even care enough about you to care about you.

HONOR: I'm sorry you feel that way.

LEEDS: But you rejoice.

HONOR: Perhaps I do. Will you tell Ron?

WARD: Why would he do that?

LEEDS: I'll say it, Ward, if you don't mind. . . . Why would I do that?

(WARD *exits to bedroom.*)

HONOR: Because you're his friend.

LEEDS: I am?

HONOR: Aren't you?

LEEDS: No! I don't even like him. In fact, I only care enough about him to find him terrifically boring.

49

HONOR: He would be hurt. He thinks you're his friend.

LEEDS: I should never have gone out with him for ice cream for everybody.

HONOR: You can't hide from me, John.

LEEDS: Listen, how would you like me to smack you right in the mouth?

HONOR: (*Sitting in director's chair.*) I might like it, it's hard to say.

LEEDS: Look, you little trollop, I don't care what you do *with* Ward or *to* Stevens. In fact, I don't care so much that in order for me *to* care, I'd have to pay off a minus caring debt so large that it would take me longer than I care to spend just to reach the point where I didn't care so I could start thinking up reasons why I might care. My only interest in this whole thing is whether or not Ward gets murdered.

(WARD *enters from bedroom fully dressed.*)

HONOR: I see.

LEEDS: Wanna bet?

(*They stare at each other. A knock at the door.*)

WARD: Hey, I know, let's pretend we're not here.

LEEDS: (*Singing.*) "My country tis of thee . . ."

(WARD *hurriedly sits at* LEEDS' *desk, snaps up a theme, studies it.*)

Get out of my chair. Come in.

(RON *enters, sees* HONOR *and crosses to her.*)

RON: (*To* HONOR.) What are you doing here?

HONOR: (*Calmly.*) Hello, Ron.

LEEDS: (*To* RON.) Just a minute.

(*To* WARD.)

I said get out of my chair, Ward.

RON: (*To* HONOR.) I asked you what you're doing here.

WARD: (*Getting up and going to* RON *with a theme.*) She finished her exam early and came back so I could go over some of the questions with her.

RON: (*Crossing toward couch, still looking at* HONOR.) Ah, well, I'll just sit quietly while you go over some of the questions with her.

WARD: (*Slapping the theme down on the spool table.*) All done.

RON: (*To* HONOR.) Why didn't you let me know you were here when Leeds got here? Didn't he tell you that I was here too?

WARD: (*Staring at* LEEDS.) Yeah, but he said you were coming right over.

RON: I didn't say I was coming right over.

LEEDS: (*He stares at* HONOR *a moment, then at* RON.) But I assumed you would because you're of a type who will come to see how a neighbor's feeling.

RON: How do you feel?

LEEDS: Within the limits of relative absolutes, terrible. Of course, if one cared to attack relative absolutes—

RON: If you don't mind—not now.

LEEDS: Perhaps some other time.

RON: Come home, Honor.

HONOR: Why, Ron?

RON: Why not?

HONOR: Because I'm supposed to be in school.

RON: But you're not, so you can come home.

HONOR: But this is scheduled as time when I'm not at home; therefore, I shouldn't have to be there.

WARD: (*Trying to salvage the situation.*) What happened, Ron, was we got sidetracked into a very interesting discussion. . . . *In fact*, why don't we ask Ron what he thinks?

51

LEEDS: Fine. What do you think, Stevens?

RON: About what?

LEEDS: Don't ask me. Ask Ward.

RON: (*To* WARD.) About what?

WARD: About . . . whether it's colder in the winter or . . . on the farm.

RON: (*Staring at* WARD, *the scientific part of his mind simultaneously at work on an answer.*) I'd say it's colder in the winter.

LEEDS: Someday when you've got a year or two, I'd be more than a little bit interested in how you arrived at that conclusion.

RON: I can tell you in one sentence: It's colder in the winter because the amount of space winter occupies is greater than the space occupied by all the farms on earth.

(LEEDS *and* WARD *both acknowledge* RON's *indeniable logic.*)

(*To* HONOR.)

I'm going home, Honor.

(*Pause.*)

HONOR: I'm going to stay here awhile.

(RON *holds a moment and then exits with as much dignity as the situation will allow. Silence.* WARD *looks to* LEEDS, *who stares blankly at him. Pause.* WARD *puts himself between* HONOR *and* LEEDS.)

WARD: (*To* HONOR, *trying to close* LEEDS *out.*) What say we drive out to the beach to this place I know and take a swim.

LEEDS: (*Returning afghan to couch.*) No thanks. I think I'll take an *Alka-Seltzer* and—

WARD: I was talking to Honor.

(LEEDS *nods understandingly but does not move. After another moment, his presence becomes conspicuous.* WARD *moves to him.*)

Do you mind, Leeds?

LEEDS: No, I don't mind Leeds. Do you?

WARD: Yeah. How bout doin the dishes or somethin.

LEEDS: (*Holding another moment, then exiting to the bedroom.*) Well!

(LEEDS *exits.*)

WARD: (*Moving back to* HONOR.) Whudduya say, very secluded, you wanna?

HONOR: Sshh!

WARD: What?

HONOR: Just don't talk to me a minute. All right?

WARD: Sure.

(*Pause; can't last a minute.*)

Should I put on my swim suit?

(*Nothing from her.*)

Want a snack?

HONOR: (*Absently.*) I'm on a diet.

(WARD *exits irascibly to the kitchen.*)

(HONOR *sits, closed into herself.*)

(LEEDS *appears in the bedroom doorway. He watches* HONOR *for a moment, then he drops two* Alka-Seltzer *tablets into a small glass of water. The tablets begin to fizz.*)

(HONOR *turns to the sound, stares at* LEEDS *a moment, then grabs up her book and purse and exits.*)

WARD: (*From the kitchen.*) How bout a no-cal cola?

(LEEDS *remains in the doorway.*)

(WARD *enters with a bowl of mangoes and sour cream.*)

(LEEDS *drinks down the glass of* Alka-Seltzer. WARD *crosses to* LEEDS.)

Where'd Honor go?

LEEDS: (*Stares horrified at* WARD.) No no *no!*

WARD: (*Looking at himself.*) What's the matter?

LEEDS: Christ, I just had a vision.

WARD: Cut the crap—where'd—

LEEDS: I did.

WARD: Where'd Honor—

LEEDS: Jesus, you know what I saw?

WARD: No, Leeds. What'd ya saw?

LEEDS: I saw myself drive over your face with one of those little automotive lawnmowers.

(LEEDS *exits to the bedroom. A knock at the door.* WARD *stares at the door a moment, wondering whether it's* HONOR *. . . or* RON, *perhaps. Decides it's* HONOR *and strikes a handsome pose, sitting casually on a bar stool.*)

WARD: (*Sexily.*) Yeah . . . ?

(*Wrong.* RON *enters, glancing around for* LEEDS.)

RON: Is Leeds here?

WARD: (*Flustered.*) Who?

RON: John Leeds. Is he here?

WARD: Oh . . . sure. Come on in.

(RON *moves to* WARD, *stares into his face.*)

How about some mangoes and sour cream?

(*Nothing.*)

I got a tangerine.

RON: I'm not stupid, Ward.

WARD: Whudduya mean?

RON: And I'm not blind.

WARD: (*With the same intonation as the first time.*) Whudduya mean?

54

RON: Just the way you say what do I mean implies you think I'm stupid and blind enough to believe that if you say what do I mean a couple of times, I'll think you really don't know what I mean.

WARD: (*Pause; then with the same near lack of intonation.*) Whudduya mean?

(*Then catching himself.*)

I mean—

RON: I mean, Ward—and I'll say it as simply as I know how: I am neither stupid nor blind.

(WARD *ponders this a moment, then begins nodding slowly, then more quickly.* RON *starts nodding to* WARD's *beat. They both nod away.* LEEDS *enters from the bedroom.*)

LEEDS: Ah, Stevens. Long time no see.

RON: (*Crossing to* LEEDS.) Can I—

(LEEDS *tries to hold* RON *off now, intuiting what has just taken place, aware that in all likelihood* RON *will insist on having a conversation with him that he's not sure he wants to have.*)

LEEDS: (*To* WARD.) Finish those mangoes so I can use the bowl to give the dog some water.

WARD: What *dog?*

LEEDS: (*A take; shocked.*) Don't we have a dog?

(*Pause; then with great disappointment.*)

Shit.

RON: (*To* LEEDS.) Can I talk to you?

(LEEDS *begins to mope around in search of his dog.*)

LEEDS: I thought we had a dog.

RON: Can I talk to you, Leeds?

LEEDS: (*He is looking under the couch, making a dog-calling kissing sound.*) Here, boy.

55

(*To* WARD.)

What'd you do with my dog?

WARD: Will you cut it out!

LEEDS: Now I remember! You wanted his fur for a bath mat!

RON: (*Trying to get* LEEDS' *attention.*) Can I—

LEEDS: Here, boy!

(*To* RON.)

Save any steak bones you don't chew yourself for my dog. Okay?

(*Whipping around to* WARD.)

If my dog's on the floor of that bathroom, your parakeet's in a lot of trouble.

(*Back to* RON.)

Is it okay, or not okay?

RON: I need to—

LEEDS: (*Peering into bedroom looking for dog.*) I know this sounds crazy, but I can't do anything until I know about the bones.

(*To* RON.)

Now, is it okay or not okay?

RON: Okay.

LEEDS: Okay.

RON: I *need* to talk to you.

LEEDS: (*Pause; realizing that the game is over, that he will have to talk to* RON.) Okay.

RON: Privately.

LEEDS: (*Crossing to his desk.*) Go to bed, Ward.

WARD: (*Returning bowl to kitchen and starting to front door. Pause; then, because he's a thoughtful guy.*) I'll go visit Honor.

RON: She's not home.

WARD: Where'd she go?

RON: (*Pause.*) Home.

WARD: Then where's she not home *at?*

RON: Home. . . . She's not dressed.

WARD: Oh. Well, okay . . .

(*Getting jacket from closet.*)

I'll go out for dougnuts for everybody.

RON: I don't care for any doughnuts, thanks.

WARD: (*Coming back toward* RON.) Well, I'll go out for dough-nuts for Honor, Leeds, and me.

(*Starts for door.*)

RON: Honor's on a diet.

WARD: (*Coming back toward* RON.) Well, I'll go out for dough-nuts for Leeds and me.

(*Starts for door.*)

LEEDS: I don't want any doughnuts. I like pizza better.

WARD: (*Coming back a step or two.*) I don't like pizza, but okay. What kind ya like?

LEEDS: Broccoli.

WARD: I'll get pepperoni, you like that. See ya.

(*Exits.*)

LEEDS: (*Pause.* RON *crosses closer to* LEEDS.) Sit down, be as comfortable as possible.

RON: I prefer to stand. . . . Will you tell me the truth about something?

LEEDS: I don't believe in truth.

RON: Well, will you promise not to lie to me?

LEEDS: I don't believe in making promises. They're self-defeat-ing.

57

RON: (*Irritated.*) Well, will you try not to lie to me?

LEEDS: If it doesn't mean telling the truth.

RON: (*Pause.*) Has Honor been seeing Ward?

LEEDS: You know the answer to that.

RON: I mean has she been *seeing* him seeing him.

LEEDS: Oh—*seeing* him seeing him. In other words, has she had coitus with him.

RON: (*Pause.*) Yes.

LEEDS: Ward says they have.

(RON *turns achingly away.* LEEDS *fights as the scene goes on to maintain his distance, to keep his detachment from this man, who nevertheless touches him in ways he doesn't want to be touched.*)

RON: Is she in love with him?

LEEDS: Oh, Stevens, for chrissake, how would I know?

RON: Well, does he love her?

LEEDS: Worships himself.

RON: I said her.

LEEDS: (*Still keeping* RON *at a distance.*) Great fondness for his triceps and pectorals; beyond that we get into murky waters. That's how much he loves her or is capable of loving anyone.

RON: I knew this was going to happen. I've been wondering what I'd do. Now it's happened and I don't know what to do.

(*Pause; waiting in fact for* LEEDS *to tell him what to do.*)

You think I'm very weak, don't you? . . . Perhaps I am.

LEEDS: (*Directly to* RON.) Listen—you're lucky. At least you're normal.

RON: Aren't you?

LEEDS: No, I'm insane.

RON: Is there any chance they haven't slept together?

LEEDS: Slept together? All the chance in the world. Ward can't sleep during the day, can't even doze, and she's never been here overnight to my knowledge.

RON: (*Heatedly.*) That's not what I meant.

LEEDS: (*Angrily.*) Then say what you mean.

RON: Well . . . is there a chance they haven't had . . . coitus?

LEEDS: (*Taking a pen from his pocket.*) Philosophically speaking, Stevens, if I drop this pen, it may rise.

RON: Is there a chance that they haven't? Just tell me!

LEEDS: No.

RON: This afternoon?

LEEDS: No. Last night when you went out for ice cream for everybody.

RON: (*Pause.*) So you knew! . . . You hate me, don't you?

LEEDS: No.

RON: But you dislike me.

LEEDS: No.

RON: (*Heatedly.*)   Do you *anything* me?

LEEDS: Yes!

RON: What?

LEEDS: I don't like you and I find you . . . *boring!*

RON: Because you think I'm weak.

LEEDS: Because you're normal.

(RON *is angry and their exchanges take on the feeling of a verbal joust, on a very low key for very high stakes.*)

RON: Well, what should everyone do—be insane as you put it?

LEEDS: Only if I could be sure of being sane. But that's not the point of this discussion, is it?

RON: What is the point of this discussion?

LEEDS: (*Crossing to counter near* RON). The point is what it is you're going to do.

RON: I don't know what to do. What do you think I should do?

LEEDS: Kill yourself?

RON: Do you really think so?

LEEDS: (*Sitting on bar stool.*) What I really think is that it doesn't matter what you do.

RON: To me it does.

LEEDS: You've got me there.

RON: And maybe to Honor it would matter.

LEEDS: I wouldn't bet on it.

RON: But even if it did matter to her, I wouldn't be here to enjoy it, would I?

LEEDS: Life is full of little drawbacks.

RON: What else would you suggest I do besides killing myself?

LEEDS: Kill Honor?

RON: Then she wouldn't be here and I would.

LEEDS: (*Rising and crossing away from* RON.) I think I see a way out. How about if you killed Honor and then killed yourself? Then you both wouldn't be here together.

RON: Leeds, I'm asking you for help.

LEEDS: (*Turning to* RON.) How about . . . killing Ward?

RON: If I killed him, I'd defeat my purpose by losing my own life.

LEEDS: There's always the chance, though, that you'd punish Honor for the rest of hers.

RON: But I love her!

LEEDS: That's what I mean, Stevens! That's relatively precisely what I mean.

60

RON: I don't follow you.

LEEDS: If you kill Ward and you don't get caught, you don't lose your life. Oh, sure, you'll punish yourself, but that's all. For all you know, killing Ward might act as some miraculous exorcism. You might cleanse yourself or become so aware of your own worthlessness that you'll save the world.

RON: (*Pause.*) You through?

LEEDS: (*Moving away.*) With what?

RON: (*Coming closer to* LEEDS).) I'd like to ask you a question about female relationships.

LEEDS: One question. About female relationships.

RON: Do you have a mother?

LEEDS: As a matter of fact, I did.

RON: Did. Oh . . . "did." I'm sorry.

LEEDS: Don't bother. It was a long time ago.

RON: Did you love her very much?

LEEDS: How do you measure something like that, Stevens?

RON: (*Impatiently.*) I don't know! Say on a forced choice basis; a whole lot, a lot, not very—

LEEDS: Oh, Jesus, Stevens!

RON: (*More impatiently.*) Well, I'm just trying to determine what kind of relationship you had with her. I mean, I assume she was—I mean, you know, did you—

LEEDS: —have coitus with her?

RON: (*Not about to be thrown off the track.*) No! Were you close to each other?

LEEDS: No. I was close to my father. I used to side with him against her.

RON: Why?

61

LEEDS: Because he scared me and she didn't. I loved her but I admired him.

RON: That's a very interesting distinction—between loving and admiring. Why did you love her and only admire him?

LEEDS: Not "only," Stevens, not "only." When I say I admired him, I mean I really admired the man.

RON: Okay—why?

LEEDS: Because he could resist feeling for other people.

RON: And so to protect yourself from a hostile world, you emulate your father. Do you think that's healthy?

LEEDS: (*Crossing to his desk, trying to end this conversation.*) Don't try to switch roles with me, Stevens! A guy like you trying to be forthright hasn't got a chance.

RON: Because I'm weak?

LEEDS Weak in the sense of great strength, Stevens. But essentially because you're boring.

RON: (*Crossing to armchair and sitting.*) And I suppose killing Ward would make me honest and interesting . . . and strong in the sense of great *weak*ness. . . . Is that right, Leeds?

LEEDS: I don't know, Stevens. But who cares?

RON: *I do!*

LEEDS: (*Crossing to* RON.) Goddammit, what is the point of all this?

RON: To make Honor not do this again.

LEEDS: *That's* the point of all this?

RON: That's the point to me.

LEEDS: And I'll bet you think that makes just a whole helluva lotta sense, don't you?

RON: Yes, I do! Why shouldn't I try to do what seems sensible?

LEEDS: (*Going back to his desk.*) Why, Stevens? Because hardly anybody else does. You're in lousy company. That's why.

Don't you know that fifty-two out of sixty sensible people are crucified?

RON: By whom?

LEEDS: The meek, Stevens, the *meek*. Don't you read?

RON: All right, but let's carry that to its positive extension: What happens to those other eight people? Those other eight people—

LEEDS: Those other eight people, Stevens, disguise themselves as eggplants and make little kids throw up at the dinner table.

RON: Are you insane, so therefore sensible?

LEEDS: I am meticulously insensible to the point of being compulsively, fastidiously sensible; therefore insane.

RON: I'm beginning to see.

LEEDS: I almost hope you're not.

RON: Why not?

LEEDS: Because I'm afraid I want you to so much.

(*Catching himself too late, in too deep; trying to jump out. Taking pistol and holster from shelf above desk.*)

Listen, Stevens, you wouldn't be interested in a little plan I've got to scare the shit out of Ward, would you?

RON: (*Ignoring* LEEDS' *question.*) Do you know what I know, John?

LEEDS: Leeds!

RON: Nothing. I don't know anything. Except that I love my wife and I don't want to lose her.

LEEDS: (*Returning gun and holster to shelf.*) You can always look back, Stevens, and remember you had twelve scholarships!

RON: John—stop it!

LEEDS: *Leeds!*

RON: *Stop it!* I don't want to lose her!

LEEDS: If you ever had her, Stevens, you've lost her.

RON: Is that really true though? Is that—

LEEDS: (*Directly to* RON.) *YES!*

   (*Pause.*)

   Yes.

   (*Silence.*)

RON: (*Rising and crossing slowly away from* LEEDS.) Then I've got to try to meet this thing as honestly as I can.

   (WARD *enters with a large pizza.*)

WARD: Can I come in, guys?

LEEDS: (*To* RON.) And just how will that be? Just how the *hell* will that be?

   (*To* WARD.)

   You're already in. What's that?

WARD: (*Coming into the center of the room.*) Pizza.

LEEDS: Who for?

WARD: *Us.*

LEEDS: You don't like pizza.

WARD: I know. I like doughnuts. But you didn't want doughnuts. You wanted pizza. So I got pizza.

LEEDS: (*Displacing his anger at his involvement with* RON *to* WARD.) I said I like pizza better than doughnuts, Ward. I said I didn't want any doughnuts, which in no way implied that I did want pizza, *which I don't!*

WARD: You mean you won't eat any of this?

LEEDS: (*Turning away, trying to get himself straight.*) Maybe Stevens will.

   (WARD *sees an opportunity to casually insinuate himself into* RON's *good graces.*)

64

WARD: Come on, buddy, we'll eat the whole thing ourselves.

(RON *looks at* WARD *with a look that says emphatically no.* WARD *crosses to counter.*)

Well, *I* don't want it! I like *doughnuts*.

LEEDS: Go to bed, Ward.

WARD: What the hell for?

LEEDS: I don't know! Because you're a *moron*.

WARD: Screw you.

LEEDS: Don't say that! It's nothing but idiomatic nonsense!

WARD: Sccreeeeew you!

RON: (*Starting for the door.*) I guess I'll be going.

LEEDS: Who the hell's stopping you!

(WARD *stands statuesquely, the pizza balanced on one hand.*)

WARD: Who's gonna eat this pizza? We're not gonna waste it.

RON: Thanks for talking to me, John.

(*He exits.*)

LEEDS: Just don't try it again! *And goddammit, call me Leeds!*

(LEEDS *holds a moment, then exits into the kitchen.*)

(WARD *remains frozen with the pizza balanced statuesquely on his hand.* LEEDS *returns with a cup of yogurt and a spoon. He takes a copy of* Saturday Review *from the top of the bookcase and sits in armchair.*)

LEEDS: What are you supposed to be—Statue of Moron Holding Pizza?

(LEEDS *sits, opens the magazine, picks at his yogurt.*)

WARD: (*Still in the same position.*) Leeds . . .

LEEDS: Ward, do not bother me at this time.

WARD: (*Breaking and heading for* LEEDS.) You're takin this pizza back and gettin a refund.

65

LEEDS: I have a feeling it will have depreciated in value. Take the money off my dresser and leave me alone.

(WARD *exits to the bedroom, depositing the pizza on the breakfast bar. He returns momentarily and crosses to* LEEDS.)

WARD: What money on your dresser?

(LEEDS *stands up, takes several bills and some small change from his pants pocket and, though* WARD's *hand is out to receive the money, dribbles a loosely measured amount onto the coffee table and sits back down, ignoring* WARD.)

(WARD *collects the money, counts it up, debates shortchanging* LEEDS, *then offers a coin or two in return to* LEEDS, *who ignores him.* WARD *plunks the coin or two into* LEEDS' *yogurt. This draws* LEEDS' *attention.*)

(WARD *moves to toy box, takes out a pair of bicycle clips and attaches them around his pants legs.*)

Well, I'm bikin downtown.

LEEDS: (*Low key.*) Yaha!

WARD: You wanna go with me?

LEEDS: What're you gonna do—walk your pizza?

WARD: (*Crossing to* LEEDS.) No, I'm goin to buy a body shirt I saw. A see-through job. Very tough on guys with good bodies.

LEEDS: (*As* WARD *starts to door.*) I think I'll stay here in case Stevens comes back looking for you.

WARD: (*Whirling around and crossing back to* LEEDS.) Whudduya mean? What'd you tell him?

LEEDS: I told him to hide in the toilet and the next time you sit down to carve up your brain with a straight razor.

WARD: You know something, Leeds: I think this Stevens thing is getting to you. Guilt over Constipation multiplied by Fear of Losing the Wager equals an Up-Tight Madman.

LEEDS: The only thing that's getting to me is the fear that Stevens isn't going to murder you.

66

WARD: That's very nice—thanks. And don't bother telling me you don't believe in nice.

LEEDS: What kind of presumption is that? Who said I don't believe in nice?

WARD: Do you?

LEEDS: Certainly not.

WARD: I'm goin downtown. You want anything?

LEEDS: For instance?

WARD: Oh, Leeds—take a day off. I got a lot on my mind.

LEEDS: Principally fungus. No, I don't want anything from downtown. But since that can't be true, pick me out a tie to go with my herringbone suit.

WARD: Gimme money.

LEEDS: Pay for it. If I like it, I'll reimburse you.

WARD: Little incentive, huh?

(LEEDS *stares at his magazine, picks at his yogurt.* WARD, *who claims a dedication to going downtown, is hanging around; he crosses to dart board and casually throws a few.*)

You're probably wondering why I'm wasting so much time.

LEEDS: Really?

WARD: I mean why I'm not putting in some more time on Honor, what with time running out and all.

LEEDS: No, what I'm wondering, Ward, is why you can't waste your time somewhere away from me . . . why aren't you putting in some more time on Honor?

WARD: Because she's sitting on the stairs out there and she's thinking. And don't ask me about what. It's none of your business—relatively speaking, that is.

(*Turning to* LEEDS.)

You know something, Leeds, I'm getting pretty good at answering your questions to my answers to your questions before you even ask them.

67

LEEDS: (*Looking up at* WARD.) And not only that, but pretty soon I won't even have to ask the original question and we won't have to say a word to each other because you'll be able to anticipate what I would ask—if I did—in the first place. And then there won't be *any* communication between us to supplement what there isn't now.

WARD: (*Crossing to* LEEDS *angrily.*) And that'll suit you just fine, won't it? Because you don't give a damn about anybody but yourself. Well, I got news for you: Whatever communication between us that stops not existing more than it doesn't now is still too much for me.

(WARD *heads for the door.*)

LEEDS: Ward . . .

WARD: I don't wanna hear it.

LEEDS: No stripes.

WARD: You said I should pick it out.

LEEDS: That was an absolute. I have to—

(WARD *slams the door.*)

qualify it.

(LEEDS *does not eat his yogurt, does not read. He sits, his thoughts on* RON, *on* HONOR, *on this "wager." He shakes off the thoughts and goes into kitchen.*)

(*There is a knock at the door.*)

Next!

(HONOR *enters. She closes the door and stands. The seriousness of whatever thoughts she was thinking while she was sitting out there on the stairs is reflected in her stance, her face.*)

(LEEDS *does not turn around to her.*)

If you're selling something, I either have one, don't need one, don't want one, was dissatisfied with my last one, haven't wanted one for years, and am not the lady of the house—or for that matter, the man either since there is no lady for me to be a man to—only a retarded child whose keeper I am—and this is an apartment which, by the way, doesn't allow solicitors, so who are you?

HONOR: John . . .

LEEDS (*Crossing back to armchair and sitting.*) I'm John. You'll have to be somebody else.

HONOR: I'm Honor.

LEEDS: That, my dear, is a misnomer if I ever heard one.

HONOR: John . . .

LEEDS: Yes, Honor, please come right to the point as I am busy.

HONOR: (*Crossing to* LEEDS.) Ron knows that I went to bed with Ward, doesn't he? And you told him.

LEEDS: And you wanted him to know.

HONOR: What makes you say that? You said you didn't care enough to tell him.

LEEDS: That's not what I said at all. You must not have been listening.

HONOR: My father's a lawyer, John. He barricades himself behind his words even better than you do behind yours.

LEEDS: I'll try to remember that. How bout your mother?

HONOR: She hates my father. He never talks to us so that we can talk back, and I think he takes as perverse a pleasure as you do in making communication impossible.

(HONOR *crosses to* LEEDS' *desk and sits.* LEEDS *does not respond.*)

Ward and I are flying down to Tijuana tomorrow morning. There's a lawyer who can have me back here and single by Sunday night.

LEEDS: You're sitting in my chair.

HONOR: Do you happen to know that Ron owns a gun?

LEEDS: Wonderful!

HONOR: (*Rising and moving toward* LEEDS.) If it's *possible*, John—if you could *deign* for just one moment to give me an honest answer, I would like to know what you think he'll really do. You know him—you're his friend.

LEEDS: I am *not* his friend! Christ, he's your husband. Don't you know what he'll do?

HONOR: If I knew, I wouldn't have to ask you!

LEEDS: Well, I don't know either. But I hope he at least makes an attempt on Ward's life, and at best I hope he kills Ward . . . and, for that matter, you too.

HONOR: Do you think he might do something violent?

LEEDS: Actually, I'm terrified he won't.

HONOR: (*Moving close to* LEEDS.) Oh, I understand you, John, I *do* under—

LEEDS: (*Rising and crossing to the desk.*) Shit—save that crap for Ward!

(*Silence.*)

HONOR: Do you think Ward and I can be happy together?

LEEDS: I have a campaign underway already to elect you Fun Couple of the Year.

(*Silence.* HONOR *moves further from him, turns.*)

HONOR: I had an orgasm last night for the first time in my life. Do you have any idea what that means to a woman who's never had one before?

LEEDS: No, but I guess it means that she had an orgasm for the first time in her life and that someone who doesn't know what it means to a woman who's never had one before doesn't know what it means.

HONOR: What it means, John, is that Ward did something for me that no other man has been able to do.

LEEDS: (*Turning to her.*) No. What it means, Honor, is that you just fucked up your whole routine.

HONOR: Really?

LEEDS: You didn't have an orgasm with Ward, because he told

70

me you were lousy, that you just lay there. Whether you've ever had one or not, I don't give a good goddamn.

HONOR: Oh, I think you *do* give a good goddamn, so I'm going to tell you. No. I haven't.

LEEDS: Well, Christ, that's real tough.

HONOR: (*Coming toward* LEEDS.) Do you know, John—it has been a certain source of aggravation to me that the few men I've wanted in my life have never had the fortitude to give me time to stop being what none of us wanted me to be.

LEEDS: Or maybe, Honor, they just saw you as a neurotic pain in the ass.

(*Sitting at desk. Pause.*)

Now, if you're through, I have work to do.

(HONOR *does not move. Silence.*)

HONOR: May I ask you a personal question? At this point, it seems only fair.

LEEDS: I don't believe in fair.

HONOR: (*Starting for the door.*) No, obviously not.

LEEDS: One question.

HONOR: (*Pause.*) Are you queer?

(*For a moment,* LEEDS *is immobile, then slowly he turns to her.*)

LEEDS: No, I don't think so. I hope not, anyway. I don't want to be. . . . The ultimate irony in my relationship with Ward is that I don't want any of my organs in any of his, or vice versa.

HONOR: Have you ever loved a woman?

LEEDS: A woman—no. I've endured several for short periods of time, but loved one—no, I don't think so. Rather fond of a girl from Greece coupla years ago. Got run over by a truck.

HONOR: (*Crossing to counter.*) That's too bad.

LEEDS: Especially for her. Loved a little girl once. We were twelve and we went steady for two weeks.

(HONOR *sees this as a breaking down of the barricade. She is careful not to take a too sympathetic approach to him.*)

HONOR: And you gave her your I.D. bracelet.

LEEDS: Yeah.

HONOR: And it made her arm turn green.

LEEDS: No. It gave her a rash.

HONOR: (*Moving into center of the room.*) Yes, I can see it. One of those big silver I.D.'s with your name in Roman type: "Johnny." No. No—you were never a Johnny. Big Roman type with . . .

LEEDS: With "Monk" on it.

(*She laughs wonderfully.*)

HONOR: Monk! Exactly! Yes. And those were the happiest days of your life, because you knew for a fact that love was forever and you had no idea that hatred is inherent to all love.

LEEDS: Very astute.

HONOR: But at the end of that two weeks she broke up with you to go steady with someone else—probably the same kid she broke up with to go steady with you.

LEEDS: And all these years I thought this was an original story.

HONOR: But you took it like a man.

LEEDS: Oh, yes.

HONOR: Lips quivering, you said, Listen, I understand—

LEEDS: I didn't say anything. I just shook hands with her.

HONOR: Shook *hands* with her?

LEEDS: Oh, yes. I used to shake hands with her every morning when I met her—

HONOR: At her homeroom. You'd be there waiting, your hair still wet and perfectly combed.

LEEDS: No—you're really getting the story screwed up now. I

72

waited for her under the cypress trees behind the toilets on the playground. And I had a crewcut.

HONOR: Ah—that's right. It's all coming back now.

LEEDS: So I shook hands with her when she gave me the word that last day, and I made a perfect military turn, marched to my gym class, started a fight with the fourth toughest kid in school and got the crap beat out of me.

HONOR: How could anybody break up with a boy who shakes hands with her every morning?

LEEDS: You, I would think, could answer that.

HONOR: (*Pause; touché.*) You do it because you want . . .

(*Can't find the right word.*)

Because you *want*.

(*Pause.*)

Don't you *want*, John?

LEEDS: No.

HONOR: (*Moving toward him.*) Don't lie to me. This is so nice now.

LEEDS: (*Turning away. Retreating into words; playing with the syntax.*) This is so nice now. Now this is so nice.

HONOR: What's happened since that little girl?

LEEDS: I've developed what seems to be an overly simplistic distaste for particular types of human relationships.

HONOR: I didn't mean to imply that many other things have not contributed to your paralysis.

LEEDS: Is nice so now this.

HONOR: What do you want, John?

LEEDS: Now?

HONOR: That's right.

LEEDS: To be hermetically sealed in sheet metal.

73

HONOR: What do you want, John? Now.

LEEDS: Not you, Honor.

HONOR: You're lying.

LEEDS: No. I'm not.

HONOR: Lying.

LEEDS: What the hell are you doing, Honor?

HONOR: (*Pause.*) I don't know.

LEEDS: What do you mean, you don't know?

HONOR: I don't know.

LEEDS: You have to know.

HONOR: It's what I don't know that I'm trying to find out.

LEEDS: Please let me be the first to confirm for you that you're going about it in a way that inspires absolutely no confidence.

HONOR: I've never imagined it to be brilliant methodology—*Jesus, why can't we stop dealing in all this language?*

(*Pause.* LEEDS *can't stop.*)

LEEDS: (*Going toward couch away from her.*) Why Ward?

HONOR: Because I can't stand him. Look—please don't bother holding my motives up to examination. I'm all too aware they won't fare well.

LEEDS: Why me?

HONOR: I don't know.

LEEDS: Stop saying you don't know!

HONOR: I don't!

LEEDS: You'll be a happier person if you stop saying that—trust me.

HONOR: You trust me.

LEEDS: To do what?

HONOR: I don't know.

74

LEEDS: *Stop saying I don't know!* Goddammit, you've been trying to drive me crazy for months!

HONOR: Don't flatter yourself. I haven't been trying to drive you
crazy, I've been trying to drive myself sane.

(*Pause. Coming to him.*)

Let's trust each other.

LEEDS: *Are you crazy!*

HONOR: I don't know.

LEEDS: What *do* you know?

HONOR: That I've been trying to get in touch with you for several months.

LEEDS: Why didn't you just tell me instead of trying to drive me
crazy?

HONOR: *Because I just found out!*

LEEDS: *Why me?*

(*Turning away.*)

Jesus, now you're making me repeat myself! Please go away.

HONOR: What have you got to lose that you can't replace?

LEEDS: Balls!

HONOR: Seems to me you're convinced you've already lost those.

LEEDS: Very nice.

HONOR: Are you afraid you'll be less successful with me than
Ron or Ward?

LEEDS: (*With a defensive, angry laugh.*) Now, why the hell did
you ask that? Couldn't you ask first if it's some quaintly
moral concern for your moronic husband or because I don't
want sloppy seconds or sevenths or twenty-thirds or whatever the hell it would be?

HONOR: I *asked* what seemed the most relevant question!

LEEDS: Well, it wasn't!

HONOR: (*Laughing the line.*) You're not being very convincing.

LEEDS: Don't laugh at me!

HONOR: But you're funny.

LEEDS: (*Turning to her.*) The most relevant question is: Are you worth the aggravation that trying to *keep* you would cause me once I'd *gotten* you.

HONOR: And you don't think I am.

LEEDS: (*Moving away from her to his desk area; absently picking up a handful of themes.*) No. Christ, no!

HONOR: (*Advancing on him.*) I see you, little boy.

(*She touches the side of his face, presses her hand there, gently turning him toward her.*)

LEEDS: Please don't touch me.

HONOR: (*Leaving her hand on his face.*) If you didn't want me to touch you, you wouldn't say please.

LEEDS: Don't touch me!

(*She kisses him, and for several seconds he almost responds; but then he pushes her away with his free hand and smacks her across the face with the pack of themes, scattering them. Shaken, he sits in his desk chair.*)

(*Pause.*)

HONOR: If you think you've just made some kind of grand gesture, you're out of your mind.

(*She moves for the door.*)

LEEDS: *Honor.*

HONOR: *Yes.*

LEEDS: I have a wager with Ward that says he can plow you within forty-eight hours of eight o'clock last night—which he did with forty-seven hours to spare—and that Stevens will either make an attempt on his life or murder him.

(*Silence.*)

HONOR: That's very amusing.

LEEDS: I'm glad you see the humor in it.

(HONOR *has exited on* LEEDS' *last line, past* WARD *who enters with his packages.*)

WARD: Hey, where ya goin?

(*Looking after her, then to* LEEDS.)

Hey, where's she goin?

(LEEDS *is mute and obviously disturbed.* WARD *peers at him, moves into the room. Then suggestively.*)

What's goin on, Leeds?

LEEDS: (*Collecting the scattered themes. Trying to get it back together.*) She's collecting in the Mothers' March against Good Health.

WARD: Yeah? —and what'd you give her, Leeds?

LEEDS: My pancreas.

WARD: (*Sitting in armchair; leeringly.*) Well well well. Ole Leeds.

LEEDS: Well well well, ole Leeds what?

WARD: Ole Leeds.

LEEDS: (*Sitting at his desk.*) Don't break your ass trying to be clever. You look much better wearing a jock than an innuendo.

WARD: How come Honor left when I came in? Wasn't she here to see me?

LEEDS: She saw you.

WARD: What was she doing here, Leeds?

LEEDS: (*Winging it.*) She wanted to know if I'd mind moving out so she can move in.

WARD: I don't believe ya, Leeds.

LEEDS: Go and ask her.

WARD: (*Rising and crossing to* LEEDS.) Move in with *me?*

LEEDS: Certainly. She said you and she were flying down to Tijuana tomorrow, that she's going to divorce Stevens and move in here with you.

WARD: Christ . . . !

LEEDS: She also said that Stevens is about half out of his mind this afternoon.

WARD: Whudduya mean?

LEEDS: What does she mean, you mean.

WARD: *Okay,* what does *she* mean he's—

LEEDS: You know damn well what she means, Ward. Don't play innocent with me, I won't have it.

(WARD *is concerned—both about how to get rid of* HONOR *and what* RON *might do.* WARD, *deep in thought, ambles into kitchen and absently begins to eat some crackers sitting at the counter. He smiles, improves the smile to a nearly convincing devil-may-care grin, and finally pulls off a laugh.*)

WARD: Jee-sus, this thing is really turning into a riot!

(WARD *rips off a laugh and* LEEDS *joins in with him. They laugh several seconds together, but suddenly* LEEDS' *face goes dead and* WARD *is left with his laughter echoing hollowly.* WARD's *face goes dead.*)

(*A knock at the door.*)

I'm not here, Leeds.

LEEDS: Let's see! Come in!

(WARD *ducks down behind the counter.* RON *enters, glances at* WARD, *who is crouched down, but visible to* RON.)

WARD: (*Using the counter for some rather deep knee bends.*) Ninety-eight, ninety-nine, one hundred. . . . Well, I'm loose. Think I'll go out for beer for everybody. See ya.

(*He exits at a trot.*)

RON: (*Moving to* LEEDS *and fixing coldly on him.*) Honor said you might have something to tell me after dinner.

LEEDS: That's pretty vague. Did she say after whose dinner?

RON: (*Coldly.*) No.

LEEDS: Hmm. Have you eaten?

RON: (*Coldly.*) Yes.

LEEDS: But I haven't. Now what do we do?

RON: Why don't I just stand here while you eat.

LEEDS: I'm not hungry.

RON: Maybe she meant after *my* dinner.

LEEDS: But you ate that.

RON: Maybe we could just forget the after-dinner part; how's that?

LEEDS: (*Rising and crossing toward the bedroom, as if to dismiss* RON.) Excellent—especially since I'm not sure what the something I might want to tell you is.

(*Changing his mind and turning to* RON.)

Could it be that she's going to fly to Tijuana tomorrow with Ward, divorce you, and then move in here with him?

RON: Is that what she said?

LEEDS: That's what she told me. What'd she tell you?

(RON *smiles thinly.*)

Come on, speak up.

RON: (*Crossing to* LEEDS.) I've come to tell you that I know what I'm going to do.

LEEDS: Good. What?

RON: The noble thing.

LEEDS: Unless that means killing Ward you've got the wrong adjective.

RON: I'm going to kill you.

(*Pause.*)

79

I said I'm going to kill you. Because this whole thing is your fault.

LEEDS: My fault?

RON: Because of that bet you made with Ward.

LEEDS: What bet?

RON: That bet you made.

LEEDS: Oh—that bet. Who told you about that?

RON: Honor.

LEEDS: (*Sitting in director's chair, trying hard to be casual.*) So that's what she told you. She's really got it in for you, hasn't she? . . . Okay, but how does that make this whole thing my fault? I mean, sure—I'm imaginative but am I *that* imaginative?

RON: No, you're not that imaginative, John.

LEEDS: Leeds.

RON: You're just that dangerous and *stupid.*

LEEDS: You don't say.

RON: No, I do say. You think I'm kidding about killing you, don't you? You think this whole thing is pretty funny. Well, you can't just go around doing these things to people.

(*He heads for the door.*)

LEEDS: What things?

RON: (*Stopping.*) *Crummy* things!

(*He starts for the door again.*)

LEEDS: Where are you going?

RON: (*At the door.*) You'll find out.

(RON *exits.*)

(LEEDS *holds a moment, then rises. He looks after* RON, *looks away, then snaps off the light just inside the wall of the breakfast bar, blacking out the stage.*)

ACT THREE

Dim lights up. RON *enters. It is seconds later. He is carrying a submachine gun. He peers through the darkness.*

RON: Leeds!

(*He moves cautiously into the room.*)

Leeds! Where are you?

(RON *looks slowly and carefully around the room. As he is about to enter the bedroom, a gun appears from behind the Little League scoreboard.*)

LEEDS: Reach for the sky, Stevens, and drop the hardware.

(RON *grudgingly reaches for the sky, but doesn't drop the hardware.* LEEDS *stands up slowly and flips on the lights and sees the gun* RON *is carrying.*)

A submachine gun! What in hell are you doing with a sub-machine gun?

RON: I used to hunt with it.

LEEDS: Hunt what—*Nazis?*

RON: (*With difficulty.*) Ducks.

LEEDS: *Ducks?* Why didn't you napalm their nests and hit 'em with some anti-aircraft fire? . . . All right, enough of this crap. Drop the gun.

RON: No!

LEEDS: Whudduya mean, no? When I say drop the gun . . . you're supposed to drop the gun. Don't you know how to play this one?

RON: *I'm not playing!*

LEEDS: (*Moving in very close to* RON, *and holding the gun to* RON's *head.*) Then *drop the gun, Stevens!*

(STEVENS *drops the submachine gun on the couch.*)

(*Moving into the room as the classic movie gangster.*)

81

Now say your prayers and gimme any last messages.

(*Clicking his empty gun.*)

Come to think of it, my gun's not even loaded.

RON: It's not?

(LEEDS *starts for the desk where his box of ammunition is. As he moves, he impotently points his empty gun at* RON.)

LEEDS: Come to think of it, I shouldn't have said that. Don't move—let me get some ammo.

(*As* LEEDS *leaps for his ammo,* RON *leaps for the submachine gun.* LEEDS *grabs up his box of ammo.*)

RON: You reach!

(LEEDS *does not reach. He stands, dumbly holding his revolver and the box of ammo.*)

Put 'em down!

(LEEDS *slowly places the revolver and the ammunition on the desk.* RON *jerks his head toward the basket.*)

Under the basket!

(LEEDS *circles slowly toward the basket.*)

LEEDS: Very clever, Stevens. I'll bet you were a whiz as a kid at "Guns."

RON: No. I was lousy.

LEEDS: Figures. Incidentally, that thing isn't loaded by any chance, is it?

RON: Yes.

LEEDS: *It is?* Well, what the hell are you pointing it at me for?

RON: Because I'm going to kill you, you irresponsible jerk!

LEEDS: Okay. All right, if you think gunning me down in cold blood will solve your problems, go ahead. Can I have a last cigarette?

RON: (*Deadly serious.*) You don't smoke cigarettes, you smoke a—

LEEDS: Jesus, Stevens, don't you know anything?

RON: *Cut that out!*

(RON *levels the gun at* LEEDS' *face and sights down the barrel. The seriousness of* RON's *demeanor must bring into doubt for* LEEDS *his safety.* RON *strains against himself, but his finger simply will not pull the trigger. He lowers the gun and walks away from* LEEDS.)

What am I doing? I can't kill you.

LEEDS: But why not, Stevens? Because I'm your friend?

RON: You don't even like me.

LEEDS: Yeah, but everybody's supposed to have one friend.

RON: Are you my friend?

LEEDS: I don't even like you.

RON: (*With ironic cynicism.*) Then you're the only friend I haven't got.

LEEDS: That's why you can't kill me.

RON: Then dammit, what *should* I do?

LEEDS: (*Finding it difficult to continue the game, but unable or unwilling to allow himself to stop and meet* RON's *problem honestly.*) Kill Ward!

RON: I don't want to kill anybody.

LEEDS: Then what are you going to do, Stevens? Do you see what great and intrinsic value communication doesn't have? We're back where we started—wondering what you're going to do.

RON: I know what I'm going to do.

LEEDS: Good. What?

RON: The noble thing.

LEEDS: Ah, the noble thing again. At last we're getting somewhere. Slow as you are, there is hope for you.

RON: Is there?

83

LEEDS: No. I don't believe in hope.

RON: Yes, so there is none. So I'm going to do the truly noble thing . . . I'm going to bow out like a man. I'm beaten and I'll accept it.

LEEDS: (*Going from mock awe to mock exultation.*) Stevens, you're a genius. That is so marvelous a thing to do because it's so purposelessly, magnificently, munificently, magnanimously *ignoble*. It's brilliant idiocy. You have achieved the epitome of weakness in the sense of great strength, Stevens, and you have practically single-handedly reaffirmed my faith in the utter innocuousness of sincerity, reason, and persistent goodness!

RON: I'm sorry to disappoint you!

LEEDS: "Disappoint!" You've practically saved my life. I was *teetering* there on the brink of feeling some sympathy for you.

WARD: (*Entering.*) You guys still at it—

(*Spots the submachine gun and grips the bag of* Fritos *he's carrying.*)

What's with the gun?

LEEDS   It's Stevens' duck hunting gun. We've been exchanging old hunting stories. Where's the beer for everybody?

WARD: (*Playing it tough.*) I didn't *get* it. I felt like havin some *Fritos* instead. So I *got Fritos.* . . . Whoever heard of hunting a duck with a submachine gun?

LEEDS: Stevens.

RON: (*Moving toward* WARD *with the submachine gun.*)

Ward . . .

(WARD *ducks out the door.*)

(*Calling.*)

Ward.

LEEDS: Go ahead, Stevens, bow out like a man.

84

(*Pause.* RON *turns angrily on* LEEDS. *Holds a moment, then storms out, past* WARD *"hiding" outside.*)

WARD: (*Enters. Swings into action, recognizing that this place and situation are good things to get away from as quickly as possible. He heads for his tennis racket.*) I gotta get packed.

LEEDS: You're not going through with the trip to Tijuana, are you?

WARD: (*Bringing his suitcase from the bedroom and throwing athletic equipment into it.*) Christ, no. I'm getting a ride to the airport with her and then I'm flyin down to Santa Barbara where I'm spendin the weekend sacked out with one of my old B-pluses. Christ, Leeds, I'm starvin for some quality.

LEEDS: (*Crossing to his desk.*) So she's going down there by herself . . .

WARD: Yeah—except she doesn't know it yet. Look, Leeds, as far as I'm concerned any obligations I might have had to her—which, as far as I'm concerned, I never did—I sure as hell don't have anymore.

LEEDS: She'll be heartbroken.

WARD: Yeah, well, she can be my guest and be whatever she wants. Fun's fun, Leeds, but when they start comin at ya with submachine guns, things are gettin a little outta hand.

(HONOR *enters.*)

HONOR: (*As if it's a quiz to which she already knows the answer.*) Well, now, if I were to give you all the choices in the world, where would you say Ron is right now?

WARD: I don't know. Gimme a kiss.

HONOR: John—care to take a stab?

LEEDS: No.

WARD: Psst! Gimme a kiss.

HONOR: (*Crossing down to* LEEDS.) Don't you wonder where a

85

man with a loaded submachine gun goes when he leaves your apartment?

WARD: No. Ya gonna gimme a kiss or not?

HONOR: (*Ignoring* WARD, *continuing right along.*) He came into our apartment and told me that he was going downstairs to the parking lot to shoot the car.

LEEDS: That'll show you, won't it?

HONOR: Now I want to know what you're going to do about it.

LEEDS: I am going to fall to my knees right here, Honor, and I am going to pray that when Stevens starts spraying bullets at that very symbol of your years together that he doesn't spray any, by mistake, at Ward's two-hundred-dollar, three-month-old, Italian, ten-speed bicycle.

WARD: *My bike!*

LEEDS: That's what I'm going to do.

WARD: *My bike's down there!*

(HONOR *turns away.* WARD *charges to the window. He has to climb onto the couch to get the only possible angle on the parking lot.*)

Goddammit, I can't see anything.

LEEDS: Get your feet off my mom's afghan.

WARD: All right, we gotta go down there.

LEEDS: Best I remain here and pray.

(WARD *looks frantically around, heads for his golf bag, starts riffling through the clubs looking for the right one.*)

I'll bet he's drawing a nice crowd for a Friday night. It's not every day that one has the opportunity to see a professor of microbiology shoot an eleven-year-old Volkswagen with a submachine gun he used to hunt ducks with. Is it?

(WARD *has selected his putter.*)

WARD: Come on, let's go!

(WARD *charges out the door.*)

LEEDS: What did he take, a wood or an iron?

HONOR: I think he took a putter.

WARD: (*Reappearing at doorway.*) Come on!

(*Exits on the run.* LEEDS *and* HONOR *stare at each other.* LEEDS *can't take it.*)

LEEDS: You can't handle a guy like Stevens with a mere putter. I'm going to take him the whole bag.

(*He doesn't though. He just exits.*)

(*Left alone,* HONOR *turns toward the window, does not go to it. She looks around the room a moment, then goes to the pizza box where* WARD *discarded it on the breakfast bar. She opens the box, deliberately takes up a piece of pizza, looks at it, then bites fiercely into it, overfilling her mouth.*)

(*Behind her* RON *enters silently. He watches her. Her mouth full, she senses someone and turns.*)

HONOR: (*Startled.*) Don't ever do that again!

(*She chews the pizza, trying to masticate and swallow enough of it so that she does not look as foolish as she does.*)

I'm sorry—that's not what I meant to say. I meant to say . . . I meant to say: Would you like a piece of pizza?

RON: (*Looking absently around the room.*) No, thanks.

HONOR: Are you sure? . . . I didn't hear any shots.

RON: The gun misfired. I haven't used it in years. So I decided since I can't shoot the car . . . I'll wash it.

HONOR: That makes sense.

RON: Sure. Can't let you go to the airport tomorrow in a filthy car.

HONOR: No.

RON: (*Crossing into kitchen.* HONOR *sits on a bar stool.*) I came to borrow an old rag. We don't have any old rags. Gotta do something about the dust on the dashboard.

(*Silence.* RON *begins a simple verbal dance of love with her. Crosses to end of counter opposite* HONOR.)

I'll tell you the truth, it's just as well that old piece of junk didn't fire. You know what would have happened?

(*She does not respond.*)

Honor?

HONOR: What would have happened?

RON: The bullets would have ricocheted all over the place and I'd have ended up shooting myself. You know that? The car wouldn't have a scratch on it and I'd have submachine gunned myself to death. That's ironic justice if I've ever heard it. And you know how much you would've cared, Honor, if that had happened? Huh? You want to know how much you would have cared if I had managed to ricochet myself to death—say, on a scale of zero through ten? Three! That's how much. No, no—hold it! That's unfair to you. Four! You would have cared a four. Four and a half at the very most.

HONOR: (*Turning to him; warmly, almost smiling.*) You underestimate yourself, Ronald. I'd say at least six and a half, maybe even seven.

RON: A seven! Wow! Not a superior care, to be sure, but certainly a middling, above-average care.

(*They stare at each other. She cannot help smile at him. He has succeeded in creating a sense between them of what they might once have had together.*)

What happened to us, Honor?

HONOR: We failed.

RON: Why?

HONOR: For more reasons than I have the energy to talk about now.

(*She looks at him.*)

Aw, don't be so glum, chum. People fail each other every day, in every way, everywhere, by the tens of thousands.

RON: But we had so much fun.

HONOR: (*Crossing to* LEEDS' *desk away from* RON.) Did we, Ron?

RON: God, yes—don't you remember?

HONOR: No, I don't.

RON: Sure you do.

(*He begins to sing the first bars of a four- or five-year-old love song.*)

HONOR: (*Cutting him off.*) I don't remember!

RON: Honor . . .

HONOR: (*In effect, please don't get to me now.*) No!

RON: (*Pause.*) How did I fail you?

HONOR: (*With a small, pained laugh.*) Perfectly.

RON: How, Honor?

HONOR: Oh, God, Ron, don't start *asking* me things like that.

RON: Honor, please . . .

HONOR: (*Turning to him.*) I failed you.

RON: Talk to me, Honor.

HONOR: Honor Honor . . .

RON: I need to know.

HONOR: (*Moving across the room.*) My *God!* Our colossal, basic, ground level ineptitude!

RON: What do you mean? I don't—

HONOR: (*Turning to him.*) *Yours!*

RON: What do you—

HONOR: Yours.

(*Silence.*)

RON: My ineptitude. Not yours?

HONOR: (*Turning away.*) Of course mine; ours.

RON: (*Coming to her.*) All right. . . . I'm sorry.

HONOR: I know you are. I know you are. I am too.

RON: I haven't been happy because you haven't, and if you've been unhappy because of me, then I'll change.

HONOR: Oh Ron—Ron.

RON: (*Angrily.*) Will you stop saying everything twice!

HONOR: Was I saying ev—

RON: You're saying everything—

HONOR: Well, I wasn't doing it intent—

RON: You said "I know you are" twice and you just said my stupid name twice! . . . Now, will you just be honest and talk to *me?*

HONOR: Honesty: Is that what you want—honesty?

RON: Look, I asked you, will you please stop saying everything *twice? Honor, why are you doing this to me?*

HONOR: Because you're nothing. Nothing! Boring! . . . Boring.

RON: I see. Well. Five and a half years down the drain just because one of the partners is boring.

HONOR: Just?

RON: I see.

HONOR: You call that *just?*

RON: Don't you understand?—I love you.

HONOR So what? What kind of big goddamn deal is that, I love you? Everybody says that like it's some big goddamn deal. *So what! I hate you!*

RON: *I'll help you be whatever you want to be.*

HONOR: *I don't want to be married to you anymore, Ronald.*

(*Silence. They stare at each other.*)

Go home, Ronny.

(RON *starts for the door. Stops.*)

RON: Are you sleeping here tonight?

HONOR: What's the difference?

RON: The difference is that tonight you're still married to me. And I know that's just quaint as hell, but if you can see your way clear not to humiliate me any further in front of that jackass you're going off with tomorrow, I would appreciate it.

HONOR: It doesn't matter where I sleep, Ronald.

RON: (*Moving back toward her.*) Yes—it does. It matters to me.

HONOR: Everything matters to you, Ronald. Everything has always mattered to you. Hasn't it?

RON: Yes.

HONOR: That's very nice, Ronald. But it's no goddamn good.

WARD: (*Entering and coming to* RON.) Hey, where were ya, guy?

HONOR: (*Returning to* LEEDS' *desk, away from* RON *and* WARD.) Be quiet, Ward.

LEEDS: (*Entering.*) Allee allee in free. Where do I get my refund, Stevens?

(LEEDS *looks from* RON *to* HONOR, *each in a corner of the stage and he knows what must have taken place between them. His sensitivity to it shows even as he continues to try to fight it.*)

All right, everybody say goodnight.

(*Crosses to couch and closes blinds.*)

RON: I'm washing the car.

WARD: Hey, you don't have to do that.

RON: I know I don't *have* to do it. I *want* to do it. I don't have any old rags. Do you have an old rag?

WARD: Sure. Take anything outta Leeds' closet.

RON: (*Ignoring* WARD, *focusing on* LEEDS.) If you have an old rag, I'd like to borrow one.

(LEEDS *moves away from* RON *to counter.* WARD *exits to the bedroom.*)

(LEEDS *stares at* HONOR. RON *looks from one to the other of them, then exits hastily.*)

I'll use my shirt. I've got seven others just like it.

(LEEDS *stares at* HONOR. WARD *enters with two rags.*)

WARD: What happened to the car wash king?

(LEEDS *stares at* HONOR.)

I brought two rags. I'm helpin him.

(*He looks to* HONOR, *who has her face pressed to the wall.*)

It's the ole philanthropist . . . protector of the downtrodden.

(*He looks from* HONOR *to* LEEDS.)

Well . . . nice talkin to ya.

(*He exits.*)

(*Silence.* HONOR *holds with her face to the wall, her back to* LEEDS. LEEDS *continues to stare at her. Finally, evidently having gotten herself reasonably enough together to leave the apartment, she starts to cross for the door. As she comes abreast of* LEEDS *though, she suddenly lets out a cry and crashes one fist down against his shoulder. He does not move. She crashes the other fist down against his other shoulder. He still does not move. In a flurry, she swings first one arm at him again and then the other. Almost metronomically, he catches in his hands first one fist and then the other. He turns her wrists back and she goes to her knees and he goes with her. He holds her viselike until she stops struggling and then he releases her hands.*)

(*She presses herself to him, her hands not around him but together and pressed by their two chests. And now he holds her loosely for some seconds before he must break from her. He moves away, in his movement a sense of desperate flight.*)

(*Silence.* RON *enters angrily, followed by* WARD.)

RON: I have no intention of washing any goddamn cars with this *putz!*

(*Seeing* HONOR *on the floor, his tone changes automatically to one of concern.*)

What are you doing on the floor?

WARD: I was just tryin to be a nice guy and help you out, Stevens.

RON: (*Crossing to* HONOR.) Come home, Honor.

LEEDS: (*Starting for the bedroom.*) I'm going to bed.

WARD: (*Crossing to* HONOR.) Right! Let's go to bed, Honor.

LEEDS: You and Honor are sleeping here?

WARD: (*Facing* RON *head on.*) Yeah!

LEEDS: Oh . . .

(*Then forcing up the old* LEEDS, *though obviously without something of the old punch.*)

. . . well, great. Can I take some slides?

(*Short pause.*)

(RON *and* WARD *hold to each other's eyes.*)

I'll sleep on the couch.

RON: Honor's sleeping at home!

LEEDS: (*Starting toward bedroom. Low key, under the level of the argument between* RON *and* WARD.) Great, I'll sleep in my bed.

93

WARD: Your choice, Honor.

RON: You're sleeping at home, Honor.

WARD: Happy to have you here!

LEEDS: (*Back to couch.*) I'll sleep on the couch.

HONOR: I'm sleeping at home.

(*Starting for the door.*)

LEEDS: (*Back toward bedroom.*) I'll sleep in my bed.

WARD: Think, Honor. *Who* should you sleep with?

RON: *No one!*

LEEDS: (*At bedroom door.*) Oh, I think *someone* ought to sleep with her. Ugly people are starving all over the world.

WARD: Who, Honor?

RON: Honor . . .

LEEDS: (*Like a kid; jumping up and down; yet in anger.*) Me me! Pleeeaase! Choose me!

(HONOR *fixes on* LEEDS.)

WARD: Hold it, Leeds! Whudduya say, Honor? Whatever you decide.

RON: Remember I asked you first.

LEEDS: (*His hands clasped in prayer.*) Dear God, please don't let there be life on other planets.

(LEEDS *rips free the afghan that covers the couch and lies down, pulling the afghan to his chest.*)

HONOR: Stay here, Ron.

(*Then with a deadly breeziness.*)

Come on, Ward.

(*She exits to her apartment.* WARD *heads for the bedroom.*)

WARD: Listen, Ron, feel free to use my bed.

RON: No!

WARD: (*From the bedroom.*) Oh . . . well, sure, I see your point.

RON: I'll sleep in the car.

WARD: What'd you say, buddy?

RON: (*Yelling angrily.*) I'll sleep in the car.

WARD: (*Entering from bedroom with a short robe, his tooth-brush, and shower thongs.*) Well . . . yeah—why not? If you're sure you don't mind.

(*To* LEEDS.)

Forty-seven minutos to go, Leeds. Well . . . night.

(WARD *exits and* RON *stands uncertainly for some seconds in the silence. He moves a step or two, looks around.*)

RON: Leeds? You awake?

LEEDS: (*His glibness throughout this scene becomes less natural, very dull and forced.*) Uh-uh. Turn off the light.

RON: What? . . . Oh.

(RON *turns the light switch off. The lighting now is low key, areas bleeding softly into one another.*)

(*Pause. He laughs. There is no response from* LEEDS.)

You're supposed to ask me what's so funny.

LEEDS: Stevens, please go to bed.

RON: (*Crossing to* LEEDS, *who is turned away from him.*) No. Ask me what's so funny.

LEEDS: No. I've been amused enough for one night.

(RON *laughs again.*)

RON: You know something, Leeds . . . ?

LEEDS: Albany is the capital of New York.

RON: . . . there's a great deal of humor here. Go ahead, give yourself a treat—ask me about the humor here.

(*There is no response from* LEEDS, *so* RON *asks himself.*)

95

What's so funny, Stevens? What's so funny, you ask. What's so funny is how funny this isn't. That's what's so funny. God, that's funny. Listen to this, Leeds, this is funny. You see, we didn't really love each other when we got married. Funny, huh? I don't know what we did do if we didn't love each other, but I know we didn't. You know how I know? My mother told me. She said, you don't *really* love each other. She was right. Now, tell the truth . . . *that's* funny! But funnier than that, Leeds—maybe forty *times* funnier than that is that I grew to *really* love her and she didn't grow to really love me. God, that's funny. Now tonight she says it's no big deal that I love her, because she hates me, and I want to point out to her that she's always hated me and that I've just found out that I've known it for five and a half years. Chuckle anywhere along here that you feel like it, Leeds. Here's the point though, Leeds—and needless to say—this is the very funniest part of all: Now she won't even *tolerate* me anymore!

(*Pause.*)

She's screwed up, boy, I'm telling you.

(*Pause.*)

God, somebody's gotta take care of her or she's gonna be in a helluva lot of trouble.

(*Pause.*)

And that's the part that I don't think's so funny.

(*A long pause.*)

What have you got to say, Leeds?

(*Pause. He sits at the desk.*)

LEEDS: Stevens, please don't sit in my chair.

BLACKOUT.

Lights up.

(RON *has moved to the armchair, but is wide awake and staring forward.* LEEDS *is asleep on the couch.* WARD *enters in his robe, carrying his clothes and toothbrush. He blows "Reveille" on the toothbrush.*)

WARD: (*To* LEEDS.) It's uppsy-wuppsy time.

(WARD *opens the blinds, flooding the room with sunlight. To* RON.)

How come ya slept there? What'd ya, fall asleep talkin to Leeds? Leeds always was a stimulating conversationalist. Haven't I always said that, Leeds? Well, gotta get packed.

(WARD *starts into bedroom.*)

RON: (*Strongly.*) *Hold it!*

(WARD *stops.* RON *has obviously been waiting for him, to confront him in some fashion. Their eyes fix on each other.*)

What have you got on under that robe?

WARD: Nothin.

(RON *wants to say something to* WARD . . . *but can't. He starts nodding.* WARD *starts nodding.* RON *turns away after several moments in which* WARD *waits for him to say whatever.* WARD *exits to the bedroom.*)

RON: (*Crossing to* LEEDS. *Focusing helplessly, lunatically on the wrong thing.*) They slept naked. He could just wake up any time during the night and look under *my* covers and there would be *my* wife naked.

LEEDS: (*Much less than pleased to awaken to this.*) It was dark.

RON: So what?

LEEDS: So when he woke up to look, it was dark and he couldn't see.

RON: (*A single-minded quasi-madness about him.*) Oh, that doesn't matter—I keep this little flashlight in my night stand. She probably told him. She probably said, "In case you wake up during the night and want to look at me naked, there's this little flashlight in What's-his-name's night stand." *What's-his-name!* How do you like that? She's already forgotten my name!

(WARD *comes to the bedroom door, partially dressed. To* WARD.)

97

Excuse me. I gotta use the bathroom.

(*He exits to the bathroom.* WARD *moves to* LEEDS *on the couch.*)

WARD: Jesus, what a night. You know, I'd even started to wonder if I could do it. But with three minutes to spare, the king, Leeds, he does it again. He wins the wager. And, on top of it, he takes her to breakthrough. Some guy's gonna be very damn grateful one of these days to that masked man. Double or nothing on double or nothing on the five hundred I didn't owe you, Leeds, equals nothing. Victory!

(*He exits into the bedroom, the champ, the Lone Ranger of sex.*)

(LEEDS *is alone a moment before* HONOR *enters with a small travelling bag and purse. For several seconds she stares at his back as he, aware of her presence, stares ahead.*)

HONOR: (*Crossing to spool table to set down her bag.*) Good morning, John.

(LEEDS *does not turn.*)

Sleep well, John?

LEEDS: (*Sitting up.*) Oh, yes. Wonderful night's sleep. Hardly remember hitting the pillow.

HONOR: You're the most insidious kind of liar. You're dead but you haven't got the decency to bury yourself. What are you waiting for in there, *Monk?*

LEEDS: Don't call me Monk.

HONOR: Your carcass is stinking up the place.

(LEEDS *exits to the kitchen.*)

(RON *enters from the bedroom and looks at her with a look at once depreciating and defensive. She stares right back into his eyes, forcing him to avert his gaze. He moves downstage, then looks at her again.*)

RON: Ward isn't finished dressing yet.

HONOR: (*Low key.*) Really?

RON: No. He's still dressing.

HONOR: That's very interesting, Ronald.

(RON *turns away from her.* LEEDS *appears behind the counter.*)

RON: Did you sleep naked?

HONOR: (*Irritatedly and perhaps even a bit loudly, as though for* LEEDS' *information, too.*) No, as a matter of fact, we didn't sleep *naked.*

RON: I don't believe you.

LEEDS: (*Coming into the room from the kitchen.*) Why don't you check the little flashlight and see if the batteries are hot?

(HONOR *turns on* LEEDS, *who stands between her and* RON *with a box of* Sugar Pops. *She stares at him and because he doesn't know what to say to her he says:*)

Sugar Pops?

HONOR: Is that pretty much the meat of what you have to say to me, John?

(LEEDS *holds on her a moment, then swings on* RON.)

LEEDS: Stevens? *Sugar Pops?*

(LEEDS *crosses to his desk and sits.* HONOR *sits on a bar stool.* WARD *enters with a small suitcase, his tennis racket sticking out of one end, and crosses toward the front door.*)

WARD: (*To* HONOR.) Let's go. I wanna have breakfast at the airport. They got an English muffin special today.

(*To* RON.)

English, o.j., and coffee, thirty-five cents.

RON: (*Crossing in toward* WARD.) What should I do about moving?

WARD: Moving what?

RON: Should I move my stuff in here and your stuff into our apartment?

WARD: Uh . . . tell ya what: Don't move anything. We'll talk about it tomorrow night.

RON: Well, I don't particularly feel like just sitting around the next two days, if you know what I mean. I'd kind of like to keep my mind occupied.

HONOR: Ronald.

RON: (*Irritably.*) What?

HONOR: I want to make something clear to you.

RON: In a minute! I'm trying to find out what I'm doing for the next two days!

HONOR: Ward's not going to Tijuana with me. He's driving to the airport with me and then he's flying to Santa Barbara for the weekend.

LEEDS: When did he tell you that?

HONOR: Mere moments after I told him I had no intention of sleeping with him last night . . .

WARD: (*Moving toward* HONOR.) Oh, yeah . . . ?

HONOR: . . . or living with him after the divorce.

LEEDS: You owe me two thousand dollars, Ward. Pay up.

WARD: There was never anything at stake, Leeds, so I don't owe you crap.

LEEDS: You owe me two thousand dollars.

RON: What do you mean there was never anything at stake?

WARD: (*Back to* HONOR, *ignoring* RON.) I was never going to Tijuana with you in the first place . . .

RON: I said, what do you mean, there was never anything at stake?

WARD: . . . let alone live with you. You know why I'm goin to Santa Barbara? Because I'm starvin for some quality, that's why.

RON: (*Slapping* WARD.) *My marriage was at stake!*

HONOR: That was mid-Victorian as hell, Ronald.

(RON *slaps* HONOR.)

RON: That's what was at stake.

HONOR: Let's stop hitting, Ronald. That's not the answer.

(WARD *retreats into the hallway.*)

RON: Well, what's the answer?

(*To* LEEDS.)

How about you? You've had the answers all along.

LEEDS: What's the question, Stevens:

(*Pause.*)

Who's gonna pay? That the question? Who's gonna pay for the ice cream, who's gonna pay for the pizza, who's gonna pay for your marriage? Somebody's gotta pay, right, Stevens?

RON: Oh, but not you, Leeds. Not you. No. Because—

LEEDS: Because that's all that's been at stake here, right? Just *your* marriage. *Right?*

HONOR: What else was at stake, John?

WARD: (*Uncomfortably.*) I gotta catch a plane.

RON: Yeah—what was at stake for *you,* Leeds?

LEEDS: (*Rising and crossing toward bedroom.*) We're not talking about me.

HONOR: (*Stopping him with her line.*) *I'm* talking about you. You can't be the perennial neuter Director of Personnel.

LEEDS: Somebody's gotta do it.

HONOR: *Not in my life!*

(*To* RON.)

Don't imagine, Ronald, that I don't choose to do what I do. One of these days I hope I'll be able to tell you why.

RON: Yeah, well don't expect me to be around to listen.

HONOR: I hope you're not.

RON: I won't be.

WARD: (*A little more insistently. But still nobody hears him.*) I gotta catch a plane.

RON: (*Firmly.*) I know what I'm going to do.

LEEDS: Christ, not the noble thing again.

RON: Israel.

WARD: Israel?

RON: *Yeah. Israel.*

WARD: You're not even Jewish.

RON: Pretty funny, huh?

HONOR: No, I don't think it's funny, Ronald.

RON: I don't care what you think. As soon as this quarter's over, I'm going to Israel.

WARD: What kind of idealistic horseshit is that?

RON: Oh, my motives aren't purely humanitarian. I have this terrific desire to kill an Arab.

LEEDS: That is . . . fantastic.

RON: Is it?

LEEDS: Yes, yes—it's mad! You're insane.

RON: Just like you, Leeds.

LEEDS: Yes!

RON: Yes, well, there's just one thing, Leeds.

LEEDS: One thing what, you maniac, you?

RON: One thing in general.

LEEDS: What's that?

RON: Being like you.

LEEDS: That's pretty general.

RON: I don't want to be like you . . .

WARD: Whaddya wanna be, a tough face-slapping son of a bitch?

RON: Shut up! . . . or him . . . or

(*To* HONOR.)

you.

LEEDS: You know something, Stevens, you make life goddamn tough on those of us down here on earth. Christ, man, I'm only in this for the laughs.

(LEEDS *speaks a two word laugh—hard, sardonic, and totally unamused.*)

Hah! Hah! Try it, it's very therapeutic.

RON: (*Mocking* LEEDS.) Hah! Hah!

(*A long pause.* RON *looks at each of them.*)

Shalom, schmucks.

(RON *exits.*)

(*Pause.*)

WARD: Let's go.

HONOR: No.

WARD: I gotta catch a plane.

HONOR: Then go. Go. You're through here. Go.

(WARD *looks from* HONOR *to* LEEDS. LEEDS *looks away.*)

WARD: (*Dallying.*) How am I gonna get to the airport?

HONOR: Take a taxi.

WARD: (*Pause; glancing at his watch.*) When do you think you'll be ready to go?

HONOR: That's hard to say.

WARD: (*Pause.*) Can anybody lend me ten bucks for a taxi—?

HONOR: Take the keys—

(WARD *snatches the keys off the breakfast bar.*)

It needs gas.

WARD: (*Dallying again.*) Got two bucks . . . ?

(WARD *fumbles in his pocket, starting to hit* LEEDS *for a couple of bucks.*)

It's okay, forget it.

(*Pause.*)

Well, see ya tomorrow night.

(LEEDS *doesn't look at him.* WARD *exits.* LEEDS *crosses to desk and sits, trying to ignore* HONOR.)

HONOR: (*Coming to* LEEDS.) Hear the laughter, John?

(*Pause.*)

If that hunk of sheet metal insists on standing there, I'm going to have to go through it.

LEEDS: No.

HONOR: No more words, John.

LEEDS: I've told you I don't want you, I've told you not to touch me, and now I'm telling you to get out.

HONOR: Words.

LEEDS: Get out!

HONOR: Words. No more words, John.

LEEDS: Please get out.

HONOR: No more words.

(*Pause.*)

Silence!

(*Silence.*)

LEEDS: I've told so many lies in my life that I no longer know when I'm telling the truth anymore.

(*Pause.*)

I'm afraid.

(*Pause.*)

HONOR: Wanna make a bet, John?

(*A long pause.*)

LEEDS: Sure.

CURTAIN

gft-6/94

xxx

DATE DUE			
2827	00825	8004	
7/96	(0)	8/94	
4/97	(1)	8/96	

3

GAYLORD
M2